The Underworld of Lesser Degrees

To My dear friend, Norman!

4-13-16

Other Books by Daniel Y. Harris

Esophagus Writ
(with Rupert M. Loydell, The Knives Forks and Spoons Press, 2014)

Hyperlinks of Anxiety
(Cervena Barva Press, 2013)

The New Arcana
(with John Amen, NYQ Books, 2012)

Paul Celan and the Messiah's Broken Levered Tongue: An Exponential Dyad
(with Adam Shechter, Cervena Barva Press, 2010)

Unio Mystica
(Cross-Cultural Communications, 2009)

The Underworld of Lesser Degrees

Daniel Y. Harris

The New York Quarterly Foundation, Inc.
New York, New York

NYQ Books™ is an imprint of The New York Quarterly Foundation, Inc.

The New York Quarterly Foundation, Inc.
P. O. Box 2015
Old Chelsea Station
New York, NY 10113

www.nyqbooks.org

First Edition

Set in New Baskerville

Layout by Macaulay Glynn

Cover Design by Raymond Hammond

Cover Art: "Lilith on the Stairs," Mixed-Media Sculpture and Installation,
Copyright © 2001 Daniel Y. Harris

Cover Art Photograph: Copyright © 2001 by Jay Jones

Photograph of author provided by Charles Weinberg

Library of Congress Control Number: 2015910554

ISBN: 978-1-63045-000-7

The Underworld of Lesser Degrees

Acknowledgments

Grateful acknowledgement is made to the editors of the following publications, in which poems in this volume first appeared, sometime in earlier versions:

Audience Magazine: "Layil Grabs Samael's Spine"
BlazeVOX: "The Melissa Oracle"
The Blue Jew Yorker:[1] "Dr. Rabbi Ari Ben Lieb Tov," "The Brooklyn Son of the Pastrami Sandwich," "Rochelle Shammas," "Elegy for a Broken Nail," "Jonah Crantz," "Atonement," "Bob Bobfeld," "A Day in the Life of Bob Bobfeld," "Seymour Rosenhat," "Excerpt from I'm a Rat: The Life of a Plasticist," "Marv Fretstein," "Excerpt from The Lamed Vavnik Killer," "Natan B. Witz," "The Hegemon of July," "Edgar William Mankewicz," "The Seven Laws of Mankewicz," "October Haverim," "E/N/C/R/Y/P/T/I/O/N"
The Café Irreal: "The Original Gasoline Totem"
Counterexample Poetics: "Reliquary Hands"
E·ratio: "24/Discomfitures," "24/Mythomanias," "24/Autoaffections"
European Judaism: "Asherah"
experiential-experimental-literature: "Para(doxa)," "Mis(ère)"
Exquisite Corpse:[2] "Kafka Six Minus One," "Drunk by 176," "Unhinged by Article 78," "Three Degrees of Kafkan Bacterium," "The J/K Hacker," "Holy Shit," "A Fork," "Hagiography of Ruined Saints," "Milena," "The First Minute Furca," "The Second Minute Furca," "The Third Minute Furca," "The Fourth Minute Furca"
FutureCycle Poetry Annual Anthology 2010: "Gatekeeper"
The Green Door: "Denaturant," "Unburiable," "Age of Incivility," "Mr. X Meets Mr. Y," "Flashmob/Worm Siege," "Ephemeris,"

---

1   *These poems and prose pieces were initially published by Daniel Y. Harris without attribution as part of Special Issue #6 of The Blue Jew Yorker, entitled "Un-Text."*

2   *These poems and prose pieces were initially published in an earlier version by Daniel Y. Harris as part of a work entitled "Seven Dead Kafkas and a Fork," co-authored with Adam Shechter.*

J. The Jewish News Weekly of Northern California: "Bestiarum," "Crocotta"
Israel Voices 2014, Poetry from Israel & Abroad, Volume 40: "Unburiable"
        (Reprinted from *The Green Door.*)
Kerem, Creative Expressions in Judaism: "Closure"
Levure littéraire: "Vocabula Amatoria"
mgversion2.0>datura: "Blue Splice," "Animula"
Milk Magazine: "The Last Man," "The Art of Corruption," "Piano"
Muddy River Poetry Review: "Grayscale," "Balladin," "Darker"
Muse Apprentice Guild: "Strains"
Of(f)course, A Literary Journal: "The Pseudepigrapha of No," "Bunker,"
        "The Half-Light of Credulity"
Orange County Jewish Life: "Inscribed"
Otoliths: "Isle of the Dead," "Les Poètes Maudits," "Cobra Lily"
The Pedestal Magazine: "Orchard"
Poetry Magazine.com: "Prolepsis," "Stasis"
Poetry Super Highway: "Sous Rature," "Mr. & Mrs. Fumian"
Sein Un Werden: "The Gimp of Redux," "Artifice"
Stride Magazine: "The Temptation of Rachel Godbot," "Hypostasis,"
        "Threnody of Reach," "Extreme," "Malaise," "Simplicity"
Tarpaulin Sky: "The Actor in My Ear"
View from the Middle of the Road IV: "The Fabulist," "Baseball"
Ygdrasil, A Journal of the Poetic Arts: "Tetragrammaton"
X-Peri: "Chameleon," "Manticore," "Onocentaur," "Satyr"

Contents

Section I. The Underworld

Section II. Lesser Degrees

for Raymond Hammond,
a friend at the core of the soul

Section I. The Underworld

Poetry begins with our awareness, not of a Fall, but that we are falling. The poet is the exemplum, our chosen, and his consciousness of election comes as a curse; again, not "I am a fallen man," but "I am Man, and I am falling" or better still, "I was God, I was Man (for to a poet they were the same) and I am falling, from myself." When this consciousness of self is raised to an absolute pitch, then the poet hits the floor of Hell, or rather, comes to the bottom of the abyss, and by his impact there creates Hell. He says, "I seem to have stopped falling; now I am fallen, consequently, I lie here in Hell."

—Harold Bloom, "The Covering Cherub or Poetic Influence"

Hypostasis

for Raymond Hammond

Faith is anemic, propane
blue—sulphur-pox:
kelvin or rankine, scaled to a thermodynamics
of absolute zero and zero
is the adiabat $S = 0$: the lapse rate
of cold transferring rapture to hoarfrost
and ring-billed gulls.

It depurifies as clot-hours circle
in arcs of new sparks, hacked
to pieces in shifts of frenzied stupor.
Signs of send rescind and cloy
and warp—scatter, splinter, bless.
Its dead were dead before undead in edits:
hack marks of corpses alive by *sous
rature*. Mentors are the gravitons
of a *petite mort*—release oxytocin
to swap spleen for on your knees.

Pray to appease Asmodai,
zombied with fog horns in the dark, hollow
hole of salted *ousia*. Antic disposition
or ontic dispossession? Never feigned.
Always canonic. To be the tilted palm,
packing in the prick-light of prayer,
Asmodai is Iago bloated as faith's
negation. Tongues are unsigned.
The haloed flecks of posthumanity
still like shards in stasis for you,
among the elect, cleaving
to a dead man's clysmic
tip of pass.

Manticore

Severs the head of the King of Maghreb,

grafts a viral stock: the jury is picked not
to court bias, philistine-sure, blood-bile
of revenge: it's a lottery, objects to no limit,

money or otherwise, prostrate—the infidel's
samadhi trades and splits, part jihad part

auto-da-fe, the rest in off-shore accounts:
salaam to the orient, *shalom*, god-speed
and *pax vobiscum*—the economy, stupid:
remember the trumpet-like voice: man-

eaters envy silk, spice and saz—palace this
you miscreant, dead from the head up.

Chameleon

Layer of Squamata—the League of Corinth
to Medici, GPS and Blue Tooth—oils

the fray in links covered with patina
and gold-leaf frames: heroes, Louvre-large,
guard fetish; the common man shall have an

arbiter picked from the lizard denominator;
roots of grass franchise grow Walt and Marat;
too late to run the contest, celebs and middle

ones: not much of a pulse to this agitprop,
survives its network flanked by topians,
who, having murdered the "u" with blue

tongues, blend with one million words.

Onocentaur

If crypto, as it were *de profundis,* slips shade

in lit crossings, then hermetic under a darker
sun, stirs the beast's reprieve: woodchips,
jaundice weed, hayfevered eroticism vis-à-vis

the upper body of a man and the lower body
of an ass: grafted roots; grim scrawl or Dante
triad, say Writ of Bedouins; aegis poetry,
when poetry mattered; the common life as

a hypocrite: we're accustomed—forget it—
the plaques the dead count for evil, terrible

good; *cogito* in *ding* sleeps through sirens,
cocks the bow and kills our spent glow.

Satyr

Cogito, ergo the origin foreclosed—flog
the paladin, the crusty skeptic, this grillwork

of muddle, leather whips and spikes—curse
the age of signs, these fetish diaphors, says
Satyr with undead erection and horse-tail;

kill hermeneutics: nothing ever is to which
nothing forms us now—hybrot skull, plasma
spine, nano heart—lay fiber below fill
for this canon of no one: the golden age

of living for five minutes has its beast;
tailored horns, manicured nails and brow;

the perfect mentor to lead us below up.

Bestiarum

Pity the wagtail, the handful of mugwort,

the two loons and swan maidens lusting
after sundogs; pity vomit, exogamy, bolts
of the sky placenta returning to Ginen
to yolk the demiurge; by default Hesiod

with Nyx and Erebus score four dwarfs,
who, through avatars, bring Indra and Vishnu
to the sixth age of Jain; Maya of the yuga stirs

Betrip to marry Pele under a bamboo reed,
chants the *Enuma Elish,* blessed by El

as Trismegistus, that Yahweh, God and
Allah joined creation powered by a blast.

Crocotta

Pliny's anatomy—the dog-wolf crest
raised above the neck, sacrum and lux
circumcised like the tongue: tilts pelvis

to walk to the hemo-shul, fibrin-church,
lipid-mosque—plain boxes, catafalques,

and caskets of *eternum*, decrescendo
in the über-after of a measured exile,
prior to the fall, on a stag's haunches,
blinded by doom; Crocotta, eye-beast

with striped gems, forgotten moniker
of misprision lures to death, unmakes
fear—prowls. A genocide in digits.

Voiceovers as hooves, the sponsored
halos, caps really—not pomp, sport

medievalism in quotes before lunch.

Griffin

Carpel of eye-rose, petalled wind of vintage

rain, *tenebrae*, pistil-soaked virgins in days
of harvest, that Gabriel plucked the unfallen,
struts the lord: *kerygma* unbinds the leper's

late jolt to sin: say lamb, goat, donkey, mule,
fish to bythos, spawns gill-ease past the horned
god, fears the son of man: bury the dead in
the sky, in the talons of a Basilica with blood-

rain, forelegs; the departed used for the skinny
mire; raptures of ingot sell glad ones news:

coeval dualism is monist, bane of *sequitur*,
that Griffin is wireless on a discount droid.

Excerpts from *Seven Dead Kafkas and a Fork*

1. Kafka Six Minus One

Dark dry-heave without lungs, eats
the brain, the torso,
                              without hunger, under siege
of k/six minus one, it curses
and blocks. The gate
is meant for you—taxon of blanks:

eschatology disfigured
by thresh in shapes of a fork,
pleads for eating k/1-k/4, k/6 and k/7—tubercular,
each an apophrades save k/5,
two tiers behind,
                              torso armored
with tentacles, molting
his cuticula in oids the law permits
to burn with envy—the second
to last, the last one.

2. Drunk by 176

One of these electrolytes—lytes, the molten lytes:
furthermore is there polymer in this drink—barkeep,
one more drink for my friend $NaCl(s) \rightarrow Na+ + Cl$—

solvation—I know how to pronounce it— the solute
of dipoles—who's talking wrong for a drink, late, we
swam this pig prairie—we were arrested by the natal,

no chaser, mixing up us aren't they—you know who
we are, National Agency for the Betterment, bet it all,
bitterment, goddamn bitter, no leaves in my lungs,

and my friend the ivil ervent, vivil mervent—barkeep,
of Written Words—there's ammonia in his ale—Ethel,
hey Ethel, changed her name from Leah, too ethnic to,

to, two here in mid-tundra, have a light—wait I mean
ethanol, two more we ald alde hyde deis in this smoky
rat-hole, my head is a rock on the floor—sawdust, spit.

3. Unhinged by Article 78

Are there apparatchiks in Montana—nomenklatura
on Oakridge Street, behind your hollow eyes, vassals
of the dead quotidian, on canvas or duck cloth? Let
the fetish out of the mimicry: escape from handcuffs,
straightjackets, cages, coffins, steel boxes, barrels,

bags, burning buildings—fool them with an open
tube of hessian attached at one end around a hole
in the back panel of a trunk, or trespass and stand
firm as if spine were pushed through skull: induce
postural asphyxia: wait. The body will turn purple.

A pair of trauma shears is coded line #777-477-987,
Section 1262, paragraph XXVII, document K. D-C
of The Registrar of Authorial Transportation, to dispel
autoerotic needs to steal identities. We, the people,
conclude a juristic call to mummification by means

of saran wrap, clingfilm, bandages, rubber strips, duct
tape, bodybags, PVC tape, red latex, and, for the sake
of historiography, embalming with organs stored
in canopic jars. Article 78 of the Statute resolved
as mummified, absolves these men of their crime.

4. Three Degrees of Kafkan Bacterium

I am a xenophobe of myself, a tangle
of tendons, penal to bury a plasmid
in the archaea of a night watchman

at the Museum of Extinct Races: here
the beetle, cockchafer, mole, sylvan
beast and half-breed, die of inanition,

the terrible atony of a golemic spool
of thread—once a people with clown
and strongman—ether lipids of ash,

grave syzygy, counted, lost: temple-
depth of stacks and a gag of wool:
bites down, the condemned to hold

the jaw in place, hears the parlograph
and holds a shovel—the crowds see
blood and water from behind glass.

5. The J/K Hacker

Nietzsche ate horsemeat
hums the (valved
voice) the decay of lying has its own kangaroo code

1. Semitic trust
2. The Greek's agon
3. The Heretic's Magdalene

Such gorgeous nonsense—full-featured
knowbots from The Department
of Homeland Worms.

I spend my time analyzing leetspeak
for terror threats—gymnosophistry

of the apocryphon—Saint Kubris
the spyware, records
all keystrokes—my

wife is Felice,
not I /we the Clanheim's
late to kevork—our

klugey fix to repair
G. Bendemann
the bug—to

4. evade the Gospel of Truth
5. upgrade genetics of a crossbreed
6. survive to judge the jurist
7. chant refuge, the whip.

6. Holy Shit

Holy shit, the gatherum at the apex—no shit
Sherlock, this batshits the bomb, scatology
of shat, glows like the shit of moray eels:

you shit medieval shitten of Norse skīta,
all for shits and giggles, shit-disturbing shitty
annuitant of fecal interest—great money,

shitloads for a scatomorphic He—not for us.
Shit in a bag and punch it, Hebrew men shit,
brings us back to the dipshittery of Holy shit:

better to be the shit, hot shit and louse shit
than the shit of fans, etiolated and crotchety
to constipated drives to buy a shit remover:

stick it up your argumentum ex stercore
tauri—money talks bullshit walks arse up
and arching, shoots the shit on a book tour:

the last taboo, the study and lust for feces,
divine coprophilia—that we aren't one of His
bad moods, but rather His dysentery bursting

after climax between davar and breshit, now
after dalet and chaf, raven and jackdaw, Daniel
and Adam to rumors of genre-making, cuts

the horizon line—not as gallinule pellets, more
as omnium of a new canonic entry this epoch's
anus has yet to release to the porcelain gods.

7. A Fork

The labile
fugitive
claw

its levity
atony

of keratins
pincers
in disquiet

incised
on the body

he lifts

black jacket
tiny

flitting
black eyes

pesky
gaunt

Pierrot
of stark
cutlery

vintage
tarsus

desacralized
girt

by thick
cords

I am
ingest

demurred
refused

to eat
tubercle
bacilli

mephitic
place

slated shy
of scope.

8. Hagiography of Ruined Saints

Max Brod's haloed dementia— skull lice:
the sayer's utensil, stainless steel—emesis
ranging from gastritis to reticular batslug

disease mediated by the vagus nerve, triggers
a cold blank stare—pleasures its seven shade
censors: f—k, c—t, c—ksuker, motherf—ker,

t—ts, sh—t, p—ss—a fork to the tonsils,
a death sentence for the martyred St. Yellow
with bastion: Brother Cadmium and his hex

triplet, Brother Chrome kissed by the chemist
Louis, Brother Gamboge spitting milky yellow
resin gum, Brother Indian with Dutch toxins,

Brother Naples the lead jaune d'antimoine,
Brother Ochre and his naked Himba, or rune
Lore mixed with Brother Orpiment, infrared

auctioneer—at the funeral, led by Herman
and Julie who lived to resettle no place near
the geography of the vain barbarity of a fork.

9. Milena

Canonical patience, my derrière, ass, the fecal institute—more like
decapod crustaceans of the infraorder known as brain dead
exoskeletons, meandering backwards, hidden under the thorax.
The women fare poorly in this regressive romp, as all his women
faired, even Dora on the last day. As if my sequel to Ravensbrück in
Martin's butcher knife was not enough, I've had to earn a meager
living as Gerstacker's aging mother, aka the decrepit shekhinah
returned
to my ultimate shame as the one legged tree.
You hegemons
of a spent trinity scoff at my umbrage,
say that I should humble myself to this titular
position among

the volatile ghosts. He said to consider him a ghost.

Now in fissures of my fatal beauty, skinned in the mock-theatricality
of a narrative—the thin scansion of iambic
feet: caesurae and pamphlets—the headless
trochee of stress: I, too, defy wit and the rules
of elision. Convey it in headlines—the fifth foot
is a dactyl, to edit a journal that speaks

for the dactylic pentameter of the people
and is released online to the silent littering
of hits. Then deport me again in bland trope,

anapestic prick to the finger of a ditch—bleeds
the stuck pig, the final foot of the spondee,
the woman in this dress: one legged tree-fork.

10. The First Minute Furca

Anonymity spreads through me like a liquid carcinogen. I'm here in pixels, there in bites, a Nom de Guerre with no enemies save myself. I have no ambition to litter the carapace of my burrowing nature. Around the proverbial fire with its orange-red flakes crackling in the black night, do I embellish tales of lost incunabula in Naron, Isfia, Hamatt Tiberias or Yaffa? I, clad in a desert-beige cloak of sacrality, nearly murdered at Dura with etrog in my bag, speak only to the quiescent voices in my head. Bestow upon me no pagan idol, Shabbat lamps nor ossuary. I was skinned alive then torn from limb-to-limb, then reassembled by virtue of some magical stitchery, only to be thrown into an inferno, where now I lay, broken on slabs. Mock me not dear travel buff, I die as I have longed to live. I am funerary art.

11. The Second Minute Furca

Were I not in the final throes of suffocation, I'd swear that these post-photosynthetic light-shapes are part cuneiform, part the language of amoebas (known to linguists as Amoebic), part Cyrillic, part Hebrew (pre-2nd Temple period)—and yet neither of these. I shame myself for so tangible a philological assessment. Dust in the lungs affects ones synapses. My last thought leads me to *Seven Dead Kafkas and Fork*—by default, by speed. My captors did say "…and through *Seven Dead Kafkas and a Fork* you go to your death." But, the *Seven Dead Kafkas and a Fork* is a legend, even a farce witnessing to the praesidium a surgery merging two torsos and two heads into one—in seven parts/shapes/voices/styles/visions/auralities/gates.

12. The Third Minute Furca

I recall holding a lance on November 21st, 1485 in Avignon. I recall following Simon the Macabee when he conquered the last resisting fortress in Jerusalem in 141 BCE. I remember eating a candied apple at the St. Louis World's Fair in 1904. Just dust in the eyes, not a memory, nor a personality disorder to distort the minute furca. When my vision clears, I look upon a beauty, burning the horizon. Cognition has named itself in the dark, replete with what appears to be an alphabet of post-photosynthetic light-shapes and cinder rooms. Not a cognition, so much as an intelligence, the future has left behind for me to see broken, anonymous, lips cracked and bleeding over a dry mouth.

13. The Fourth Minute Furca

Shtetl life is no fin de siecle Bohemia: Volkovysk is no Prague. My
Kafkan country doctor never spoke of phylacteries. I have given birth
to myself, the Flaubertian eidolon casting the spoils of fellatio against
the hard clinamen: our father who art in heaven-all-too-human
inseminated by paraphilia. We are brothers—kneel as we do beneath
the tribal palladia to ingest the drone notes of our irrumatio.

The Gimp of Redux

Necromancer snakes or an équipe of homunculi?
In the octagonal terminus coyly
dubbed "St. Replace Aller," the acolytes
gather to declare allegiance to a primordial
nothing named ENTROPOID.

They gyrate and twitch to the droning
dissonant beats of *Repeat Murdock,*
an oldschool DJ ensemble of hybrid bots
with built-in tear ducts. Piles of clothing
are burnt in effigy. A 1976 Chevrolet Caprice
Classic Landau Coupe is dragged with dental floss

by a bald man without a jaw. Laughing
tracks intermittently drown out *Repeat Murdock.*
Behind the casement window, below chipped
beige paint, the next in line zips his leather face.

Les Poètes Maudits

Avec l'assentiment des grands héliotropes.
—*Arthur Rimbaud*

Innards culled for goths of the *virile*
membrum, the maudit décor, red
and black puissants *de la terre* with

swells of flecked blue, conspire to
mock the agony of hands, albatross
and crow lit by haloed skulls, reach

the cipher casting a hook in search
of lost wine, at the Chat Noir, dips
plume in laudanum to séance *fin*

de siecle specters of the Paris quay
with espaliers: erect grin of Satan,
Delphine on a scented sofa, add

to this rancor, alchemy: Rodolphe
Salis's *iriso subversive* below a
wrought iron chandelier in frock

coat with copper beard—below
the accursed spirant, the green
haze of absinthe's steady drip.

Isle of the Dead

after "Isle of the Dead," Arnold Böcklin, 1880

Steals the corpse and faces the watergate
with its sharp islet and steers a gaunt, white
figure maneuvering its rowboat from the

stern. The oarsman's yellow, fetid hair
drooped over his red ears, hears the faint,
whisked laughter of waves resist brown

oars. Cypress trees hemmed in by ports,
engrave the rocks, are molested, cold,
blue-black by salty, sea air with the gray

hum of stench rot rising with bony gulls—
soils canvas with mustard chiascuro, and
now, emptied of color, sees itself on the

green hill with the crescents of wolf eyes.

The Art of Corruption

after "Narkissos," Jess Collins, 1959

Dear Jess, a crack in the armature layered over a thousand
heads. There are no/all dimensions here finely cut to sky the
alchemy of a religion of scissors. Your vision was forever

shaped by the cubists. Ernst and Cornell bothered you most.
They were the canon from which you cast your spell. You ate
Duncan's words. History severs its mechanical reproductions

reconstituted for the coffee table where your future is intact.
I will never see the world again as it was convinced of its
narrative strains and dogmas. The numb are resolute and grow

more resolute. We've even lost a dimension. I believe we're
down to two but I frown with high spirits. Others more carcino-
genic in their appraisal than I say one and they don't mean

"the one—" one dimension, one manner of speech, one day of
memory, one type of person, one language, with one principal
mode of expression, one reaction, one emotion. I won't burden

your dead sleep with the media. You know how they have
turned the entire population of the United States into one person.
"An American," Jess. I still see two dimensions. One dimension

daily reinforced by a mass market of media and the hegemon.
The other, where boredom bears its rude consort, we reside,
we specters of image and glut, we revolutionaries of distance.

What about the third, fourth and fifth dimensions? The latter
slips into finger blades and returns as cult classic. Three and
four are recomposed in chemical cityscapes of homoeroticism,

are trashed, dear Jess. I saw one the other day, one of the three
or four next to a yellow burger wrapper. I thought of you. I
thought of hundreds of cut seamless images inside the yellow

wrapper. Here was Botticelli, Vermeer, Michelangelo, and of course you Jess, the maestro conducting a symphony with a scissors for a baton and fries. I have ten pairs of scissors Jess.

I had only one when I saw my first Jess. A Fiskars. I have kept that pair though it is dull and rusted, the orange loops bows to the metal ring next to a clevis pin. Most affectionately yours.

Blue Splice

for Walter Ruhlmann

Icy blue cyanosis—in my zone, a rare
blue dahlia in a saucepan of herring
with blue-back and the discoloration
of a bruise, at loggerheads. At once,
blue pills, blue pencils, *Blue Danube*

and lilac, or blue veins, blue moods,
the rarefied blue disk longhorn beetle,
pale compared to blue-mold in the blue
light of a freezer icing a copy of *The Blue
Octavo Notebooks*, a postcard of Picasso's

Les Noces de Pierrette with a list of *Der
Blaue Reiter* on the back, Turkish tiles,
several plastic blue jays and lapis lazuli
costume jewelry. Alone, there's the blue
skin of cold built as psychosis of spent

haunts, left to sequence, slated to be
strung together like blue pearls: beryl,
cobalt, damson, cadet and periwinkle,
tinting the bluish shades of verdigris
toward the final bleached blue of me.

The Half-Light of Credulity

But it was precisely because it was an empty game that Baudelaire enjoyed it.
Nothing gave him a greater sensation of freedom and solitude than empty,
sterile acts which produced nothing, a phantom evil which was pursued and
suggested rather than realized.

—*Jean-Paul Sartre*, Baudelaire

Dear Yahweh, the unformed is trussed up
as a sacrificial droid, waiting to speak
the rupture of your epochal stint in clay—
ruptured and sutured, speaking the fissure
within divinity but not divine, nor even dim
scintillae of what is hazard and named *Ayin,*
to quell the aegis pleas for a place, a time,
a people, a craft. My letter is preemptive.
My prosody, the result of a blur in the gleam
of irreverent requests to change names
and be spectral like a Griffon Vulture.
It's my only chance at progeny. My fault!
I remember Abram from Ur of the Chaldees,
remember the boils spilling bile below a low
sun firing at the edges of a resolute blessing.
I remember the back of his eyes, that "Father
of a nation, uniformed in dark allegiance
to a *Book,*" above staves cursed by vows
to taunt the nimbus of blue sapphires.

What's in *The Book?* Where is the "cavernous
spell" that has coerced a thousand generations
of devotees and radical unbelievers colluding
in despair and dry cynicism to stress the precise
date of its death? I, pursuant to protocol to provide
clear access to *The Book* say, "I am that I am alone,
and have no life without you." I erase traces
of theogony. I replace exegeticals with rebuses,
desperate to identify sinews that connect

the burdens of our names. "A," the *Alef*
lured from the *Resh* of my name, produced
The Book. Abraham/Adam—Rayin/Yahweh:
the fourfold tongue cast in a diurnal panache.
The Book is a vessel containing the point
from which nothing has cracked to extend
out of itself. *Alef:* the first and last point
at which zero is filled with a chimera/corpse,
hollow body, the last of the slurred clangor.

"Be like me O pods of simulacra, but if you
are, I, the Lord of *The Book* will terminate
you and watch." Tribe names end with "M,"
Matronita, the "Mem" in tears created a glare-
eyed Leviathan, Eden's oily conduit to a
cemetery of dead letters. We are the perco-
lating letters of names without end, speaking
with circumcised tongues, babbling to divide
identities from the mystic equity of response.
Here's one. When I repeat your prayers to walk
"a path beyond the powers of the Creator," I
tremble in myself, a private anguish, to find
myself in a room full of mirrors, surrounded
by people who all have my name, who all look
like me—me the fissure, the dark chasm,
groping for a rib, which is *The Book*—to
count the letters, the veins—the hapless
jubilo of distress, that I, Rayin Lev,
make of your monodies of trust.

Excerpts from *Un-Text*

1. Dr. Rabbi Ari Ben Lieb Tov

Dr. Rabbi Ari Ben Lieb Tov was born in Brooklyn. He received his rabbinic ordination and doctorate of Hebrew Letters from the Hebrew University in Jerusalem, where he chaired the department of Talmudic Forensics, before returning to his native Brooklyn. Dr. Rabbi Tov is a fellow of the Society of Fellows of Harvard University, and taught at New York University, Yale University, Cornell University, Stanford University, The University of Paris, The London School of Economics, The University of Copenhagen and Stanford University. He is currently Professor of Old Testament at the Union Theological Seminary in the City of New York. He is the author of numerous books including *The Mishnaic Epidermis* (The Jewish Publication Society, 1968), which was nominated for a Nobel Prize, *Acid Reflux, or the Sociopathology of a Butcher's Son* (W.W. Norton & Company, 2004), which was awarded the coveted Israeli Prize for Literature, and *Thirteen Ways of Looking at a Hasid* (New York University Press, 2005), a gastronomic long poem, parts of which were published in *The Jerusalem Quarterly*.

The Brooklyn Son of the Pastrami Sandwich

Delivered out of the raw condiments of salted brine,
I am the Brooklyn Son of the Pastrami Sandwich—smell
of garlic, coriander, black pepper, paprika, cloves,
allspice, mustard seed: apron of the shibboleth
and stench of the butcher's knife I should of used
on myself. To slice and be sliced, these flaps
groan like cannibals, brown mustard smeared
on Christian kids—my father's neighborhood
secret, first lured by caramelized apples then
trapped, stripped, suffocated, drained of blood,
urine, semen, skinned and smoked. During
Pesach, the number of dead Christian children
rose to over two hundred and seventy five. My
father gave a fifty percent discount to parents,

throwing in a ounce of slaw, dill pickle and first
dibs on their children's skin. Me? I prefer a French
roll. I stalk the streets like a rabid wolf hunting
young meat. I attack from behind, kill quickly,
recite the Kaddish (at times in two part harmony),
and wrap the delight in a tallit. The body dies
black-purple, strangled by teffilin. In my kitchen,
I sever the head from the neck, sever the feet
at the ankles, hands at the wrists and begin
to slice skin from the thighs and back. My
butcher's knife is my father's butcher's knife,
blessed by the great Satmar Rebbe. Baruch
Hashem, my children are gone. They were
tasty. No one tastes like them. I suffer.

2. Rochelle Shammas

Rochelle Shammas is a cosmetologist with long red painted finger nails fashioned to emulate the ancient Egyptian Queen Nefertiti, the wife of King Akhenaton. She has a station at Catskills Beauty & Nails, where she serves an average clientele of twelve per day. When not waxing her peripatetic cosmetology acumen, i.e., esthetics/skin care, nail technology, barbering, electrology and laser training, Shammas enjoys the works of James Merrill and Constantine P. Cavafy. In fact, during spells of demiurgic inspiration, she has been known to write excerpts from Merrill and Cavafy on the heads of her bald clients. They have been known to send flowers and chocolates. Of these gentlemen and in some cases gentlewomen suitors, a certain Professor Reginald Lipschitz had a particular attraction to Ms. Shammas and invited her to attend an exclusive poetry conference at Yale University in which he was chair. A deeply repressed and fragile wordsmith, she reluctantly accepted Professor Lipschitz's invitation with a coquettish wink. On the flight to New Haven, Ms. Shammas confessed that she dabbled in poetry. Gazing at her succulent lips and large breasts nicely packed in a summer dress, Professor Lipschitz asked Ms. Shammas if she would like to read at the conference. The following poem "Elegy for a Broken Nail" has been anthologized in *Dust, Mold and Platitudes: A Poetry Conference at Yale University* (Yale University Press, 2008).

Elegy for a Broken Nail

A broken, red cracked nail: a song from sleepy love,
me from my sex, myself, connected to
a head, a body—professor I wield cleavage,

wink, wafer-thin in a summer dress; slice,
survive into new life. Or do I?

And you, the other, bulge in a corner
glaring a threat or promise.
I long to write on your pole.

Ram me, I add a false nail,
testing the bond, I scratch red to a sore.

3. Jonah Crantz

Jonah Crantz has published 75,613 individual poems. He works for the City of Des Moines Public Works Department, Defective Sidewalks Division. When not surveying tarmac and publishing poetry, Mr. Crantz enjoys reading the works of Shul Hemorvitz, the Polish 18th century mitnagdic Rebbe who was beaten to death and eaten by the Cossacks.

Atonement

The great Reprover has ended His vivisection.
The sulphate day is over and the drones are cloning.
How pardoned all that has been purged was probate

by us, how maggidic all that should be said. Gray
prophets will go in phlegm. It smells, remove it.
The devourers will hazard the crunched shellac.

The sentence is stark. The occlusion, a dip. Wrapped
and sustained through the davening of weathered
droids, for we, I demur, are the dusty relics flung

in the wake of The Ancient of Days. I remain like
an outdare with ten pens and two fingers: the rabbi
of loss with his consort, the shekhinah strapped

like a dominatrix, immortal with an itch. Creature,
the man-beast, golemic with the cranium of a pill
bug, deliver me from the fetish of response. Amen.

4. Bob Bobfeld

Bob Bobfeld is not acclaimed. He is uniquely without distinction, merit, achievement nor individuality. Mr. Bobfeld possesses no qualities, is average in height, weight, physical appearance, dress, manner and style. No one has ever recalled meeting Mr. Bobfeld. He leaves no impression. He has no accent when he speaks in that audible mix of monotonic affirmations and niceties. Mr. Bobfeld worked in the accounting department of the First National Bank in Brush, Indiana. For twenty-seven years Mr. Bobfeld was never late, never sick, eating lunch at twelve and leaving at five sharp. He never received a raise nor change in title. He remained faithfully "Bob Bobfeld, Accounting Department." When he retired his co-workers simply said that his position had been vacant for years and that it had been very difficult to fill. Bob Bobfeld died unpublished. He had no aspirations to write anything. In fact, his mother, who claimed that "Bobbie" died in childbirth, never wrote anything. Following his credo that "even the worthless among us deserve to be dissected," Bob left the following snippet on his kitchen table, before taking to his bed to die.

A Day in the Life of Bob Bobfeld

5:30 am—My head is the size of a dumpster.
7:00 am—One ant. Two ant traps.
8:17 am—Reorder pencils.
9:29 am—Light right foot on fire. Same thought everyday at 9:29 am.
10:32 am—Must work on having another thought. Buy the manual.
11:52 am—What's the time?
12:43 pm—Cuticles provide hours of pleasure.
3:00 pm—Reorder the thin rubber bands.
4:12 pm—Is headcheese really brain?
5:00 pm—My head is the size of a dumpster.

5. Seymour Rosenhat

Seymour Rosenhat, acclaimed international artist, Dip. Arch (Dist.), M. Arch (UXL), was born in 1980 in Lumox, Texas. He studied Architecture at the RWOP Zychen, Hungary, the University of Applied Arts in Manheim, Germany (master class of Dogmar M. Vix), and finished his studies at the Bramlett School of Architecture. (Distinction in Design, Commendation LUDITE Silver Medal 2001; Winner UBER+ prize 2001). He has worked as a design architect for Blob Cumelbled in Minsk. He collaborated with Bagel Floats on various projects (Sactacity, Venice Biennale 2008) and works as a consultant for several offices in Lumox, Texas. Rosenhat has taught architecture at universities including London, Fresno, Tour and Buttingham. He runs BS23 at the Royal College of Art in England together with Billy Bob Lazzi. Rosenhat is also curating the International Below Architectural Lecture Series at the University of Kruzia with Denny Itsu, and is a Unit Master of the first-year programme at the Architectural Association.

Excerpt from *I'm a Rat: The Life of a Plasticist* (City Lights Books, 2008)

Suck the acerbic stench from chiascuro—leave the pallid face exposed to a cerulean wind—the focal point of the chromatic palette with burnt umber—the ceaseless angst—the hand of scale with its wiry rodentia—bastard muroid—moldy slice of Munster—the plastic tibia to chew raw—model to bone—twittering machine—Medusa's raft with clots—the blotted lever—clever plastic underworld—to tumor the angling light which drains the rustic cabin on the lake where an unidentified creature roams—Styrofoam's biodegradable malaise—artflow sabotage annihilates the second commandment—the graven substitute people for cutlery and healing warts.

6. Marv Fretstein

Marv Fretstein is an aspiring serial killer. Among his numerous influences are David Berkowitz, the M.O.T .44 caliber killer, aka "Son of Sam, Ted Bundy with his degree in psychology from the University of Washington, Jeffrey Dahmer, the punk rocker who worked at the Ambrosia Chocolate Factory and John Edward Robison, the "cybersex killer." Mr. Fretstein calls himself the "Lamed Vavnik Killer." His intent is to seek out the thirty-six most righteous people of his generation and murder them. Since May 1, 2009, Mr. Fretstein has killed twenty-three people including Menachem Mendel Schneerson, ("The Rebbe") who, contrary to medical consensus, didn't die of a stroke but rather was poisoned. Excerpts from Mr. Fretstein's evolving manuscript, *The Lamed Vavnik Killer,* have been published in *National Geographic, The National Inquirer, People Magazine, The Nation, Playboy* and *Better Homes & Gardens.*

Excerpt from *The Lamed Vavnik Killer*

As an entropic concept of vile disproportion, the number 36 (their heads kept as trophies on stakes in the cellar) is soaked in mustard gas. It is said that at all end times (when the eschaton is named "Marv") there are 36 blood-sucking sacks of scatological skin pods in the world, and that were it not for them, all of them, if even one of them was missing, the world would continue to tick in fumes of yellow-beige banality. The humdrum. The quotidian. The tedium. The routine. The clichés. The two Hebrew letters for 36 are the Lamed (gun shot, knife, strangling, poisoning) which is 30, and the Vav (car bomb, arson, kidnapping and torture, hit-and-run, bludgeoning) which is six. Therefore, these 36, the Lamed-Vav-Tzadikim-Vampires of daily life are being killed by a charming apprentice in order to tilt the planet off its axis and annihilate six billion people.

7. Natan B. Witz

Natan B. Witz, M.D, Ph.D, is the author of fifteen books, including *Declensions of Rasp* (HarperCollins, 2005), *A Year of Dysentery* (Harvard University Press, 2001), *Below the Knees* (Houghton Mifflin, 1999) and *Fanfare for a Vintage Beater* (Alfred A Knopf, 1993). His poems, stories and essays have appeared in *The New Yorker, Vanity Fair, Poetry Magazine, The New York Review of Books, Times Literary Supplement, Yale Review* and *The Paris Review*. He has been named a Guggenheim and a MacArthur Fellow. Dr. Witz has been awarded a National Book Critics Circle Award and was winner of the 2006 National Jewish Book Award in the Category of Jewish Thought given by the Jewish Book Council. He is the Alma Mahler Professor of Intracellular Parasitism at The John Hopkins Hospital, President of the Board of Directors of Congregation Beth Ezra and Past President of United Jewish Communities.

The Hegemon of July

All spring I smell them
mangling in the blight,
outlifting me from spit
to stake in my abbatoir,
a scream among the exsanguinations,
a signal pierced from the slaughter,
a rack of flesh skewed
in the thicket of a carotid artery.
Now that the nights are aortas
and the phrenic splayed,
I should have removed the down
pullers in a torpor of blood
slashed to the jugular
before the head hunters.
Make it so. In the collusion
of dawn, as if prostrate to curses
that soiled the last man,

these phobics appear
through a slit in holy writ,
in the flames of white fire
on black fire and skin welts,
mangling head-off, hybrids
in volumes of sticky bile.
I put myself out of misery,
the fine vein grit of my skin.
After all, I am the king,
covenant signer of my
touch who funnels
a herd.

8. Edgar William Mankewicz

Edgar William Mankewicz is former Chief Investment Officer for Merrill Lynch. He is a paranoid little man with thinning hair and chronic body odor. He talks to himself and can be seen taking swings at the air. He lives on a diet of tuna and warm water. Lukewarm water. Flat water. He has never married, nor for that matter dated. He rides the bus. One day in order to augment his meager biographical statement, Mr. Mankewicz attempted to lie in front of a moving bus. To his dismay, he realized that he was watching television. Currently, Mr. Mankewicz writes an occasional op-ed column for the *Wall Street Journal* under the name Rick Dick.

The Seven Laws of Mankewicz

1. The quintessence/ur/primordia of the Mankewicz scheme is that, I, Edgar William Mankewicz use the money, liquid and futures I receive from mannequin investors to pay extravagant rates of return to early clonic investors, thereby inducing more uber investors to place their money with me in the false hope of realizing this same extravagant rate of return themselves.
2. This works only so long as there is an ever-increasing number of mannequin, clonic and uber investors coming into my scheme.
3. To pay a 100% profit to the first 1,000 prehensile investors, I need the money from 2,000 prepubescent investors.
4. To pay the same return to these first 3,000 pigmy goat investors in the next round, I need the money from 6,000 new pomade investors.
5. If all the meat puppet investors stay in the scheme, then I will need 18,000 new quagmire investors to pay off the first 9,000 hopeless sacks of manure investors.
6. If all the synthetic investors stay in my scheme, the number of digital investors participating has to triple with every round of postpartum investments.

7. In my William Henry Mankewicz scheme, starting with only 1,000 reptilian investors, after the 15th round the number of hybrid investors will exceed the population of the earth.

9. October Haverim

October Haverim is an iconoclast, a droidic übermensch who manifests within himself the true nature of Friedrich Nietzsche's "Zarathrustra." Mr. Haverim sports a tattoo on his arm which says "God is dead and I have killed him." He embodies the very core of Internet media, being himself one of the inventors of digital deoxyribonucleic acid known by the trade mark DDA® and accessible at www.dxdya.com. DDA® has three rivals: the Library of Congress, the Vatican and Microsoft—each are strategic targets for what Mr. Haverim charmingly dubs "creative usurping." DDA® exercises the privilege of translating every document that it posts into the world's 6,700 languages. In fine, DDA® releases a minimum of 6,700 unique issues per minute or (525,600 x 6,700 = 3,521,520, 219 issues per year.) Mr. Haverim's rivals have called him "a plebian masquerading as a parasite" while sentencing him to a ceaseless barrage of viral Spam. Bloggers lacerate his character and vulgarity on a daily basis. He is simultaneously listed at the head of America's Most Wanted, wanted by The Hague War Tribunals, boasts two fatwas and the honor of having a nuclear weapon intended for him alone. On Saturday, May 23rd, 2005, Mr. Haverim, identified at that time by approximately 1,117 separate aliases, vanished. No further issues of DDA® ensued. In fact, the very last issue released at 11:27 am on May 23rd, 2005, remains frozen in cyberspace at his distinctive Url. The following hyper-extended text with its savage metalepsis can be viewed on his homepage.

E/N/C/R/Y/P/T/I/O/N

Limbic behavior occurring at the daemon bifurcation: the attract-ing/de-acting fpoint "collides" repelling period q-cycle –1.401155 or –0.1528 + 1.0397i#@endtime, volution function discrete/waxy non/post/ur/linear dynamical system: *lap numbers* of the iterates X-ray— paramour diffraction and scattering points tilt 995-223156 to damage cyber mortification and imposture bromide, dragging of the alias, septic, for the latrine heads and homunculi posturing chariot mucous, a Lord Protector shredded limb by limb: raven.

Mr. & Mrs. Fumian

The counter man admitted that it might have slipped his mind.

— *Rick Lupert*
I Am My Own Orange County

Mrs. Fumian packs salad tongs, drags Mr. Fumian to a picnic.
He sips gooseberry wine, eats deviled eggs, *choucroute garnie,*
boysenberry tart and legumes sprinkled with figs. He asks her
to baste his pasty brain. He would rather be anywhere but on
a gridiron. "No reprieve for soured prigs pickled in the brine
of mango enchiladas," she blurts and stares. *A la carté* or *table
d'hôte* with *prix fixe?* If not, then he escapes. He hurls himself
into a construction site finally getting revenge on the random
betrayal of the obscure and screams "sluiced without hands—
bloody metrical feet" to deafen the pop rage of his irreal mind.
He texts: "Unapprove. Unendorse. Unclap. Unsign. Undelete.
Unerase and unclip coherence." He devolves as alien specie
with three sets of ears and a defective derrick—the gestured
clamp of his beret as a rivulet of rebar. His name is Fumian
with an "F" as in fluke for sophistry were phonetics his *lingua
franca* and Dr. Frank-N-Furter his alias. "We're Tristan and
Isolde played by Ludwig and Malvina Schnorr von Carolsfeld,"
chimes in Mrs. Fumian." "Weren't you naked and licking dark
chocolate sauce at last glance?" ribs Mr. Fumian to three obese
men dipping triple cheeseburgers into vats of mayonnaise. Scorn,
rage, furious outbursts and potions beside a burning brazier dead
with Fumian on his lips. This is a Bluetooth opera curled on a
spare ear sounding hard turf with a *si bémol.* "Now everyone sing
Ornithorhynchus Anatinus here at the Cobalt Café," waxes Mrs.
Fumian in June prior to the arrival of a lost tribe of Naqshbandi
acolytes speaking of Albrecht Dürer's ship in *Stultifera navis* by
Sebastian Brant, published by J. Bergmann von Olpe in Basel
in 1498. Now that's spin. Woodcut or styrofoam nose ring? Gas
blasting alert and a non sequitur to add to an otherwise less than
stellar performance. Were such a thing true, exegetes would blurt
out umbrage and madly eblast retorts to Emperor Maximilian,

Thomas Murner, Konrad Peutinger, Willibald Schott, Johannes Reuchlin, Beatus Rhenanus, J. Wimpfeling and Ulrich Zasius, whom all read at the Open Mic and drank Diet Cokes. Later, chauffeured in gridlock by a mock Danton waxing *The Reign of Terror* on the 101 out of LA, the Fumian's play Charlotte Corday and Jean-Paul Marat singing hip hop versions of *The Brady Bunch* eating seasoned curly fries with Cheeze Wiz.

The Original Gasoline Totem

Fragment from THE SAYINGS OF PETROLUS

Petrolus of the Gasoline Totem speaks to his disciple, Saint Hydrocarbon:

"You among the chemical seraphs of this celestial refinery speak the speech the way I pronounced it to you, gasingly on the tongue. Your crude oiled tongue bears conversational daft. Fumes, all fumes."

Saint Hydrocarbon divides and conquers his disparate parts. Benzene, Toluene, Naphthalene and Trimethylbenzene are sainted. Saint Benzene leads the procession to Saint Toulene's dismay. Saints Naphthalene and Trimethylbenzene carry pump handles. From this day forth, Saint Hydrocarbon is known as the Catalytic Reformer.

Petrolus of the Gasoline Totem speaks to his disciple, Saint Hydrocarbon:

"You among your Crude Saints, raise your Octane Level and Sacrifice the Anode, I, Petrolus of the Gasoline Totem, name ZOROGASTRIAN."

Saint Hydrocarbon sanctifies Zorogastrian and the earth burns for a thousand years.

The Discovery

Digital archeologists, excavating a remote region of the Internet, burrowing through layers of volcanic html, uncover, to their dismay, an ancient Totem with an inscription entitled *The Sayings of Petrolus*. It is surmised that this totemic remnant, important as the discovery of the so-called "Copper Scrolls" containing fragments of Essene Wisdom in 1947, is the sole remnant of an ancient people called the "Petrolites." The aforementioned text was written in Petrolan, an Indo-European amalgam of the Demotic, Phoenician and Hebrew languages, by Petrolus, circa 2nd CE.

"*The Sayings of Petrolus* were discovered inscribed on the pump handle," said the lead archeologist. "We're lucky, plain lucky," he added, sensing a Nobel Prize. The ethos of Petrolite civilization, its socio-politics, relations to its surroundings and advanced knowledge of fossil fuels, are now being debated by teams of scholars and oil company executives.

59

The Actor in My Ear

...to succeed in shifting the signified a great distance and in throwing, so to speak, the anonymous body of an actor into my ear.

—*Roland Barthes*
The Pleasure of the Text

Scene I.

Disfigure the spine of the prattling
text—the makeshift
blank, the pause,
                    staid
and violent, touched
and shoved down to a single word:
unit of milky phoneme to a speck
of flaw—"actor."

The poem is a farce acting its way
back—foretells
its sociolect
                    on stage/backstage:
the one tamped down
is hollowed out.
                    Method is rendered
friable and applied to the face,
that surrogate loss of verbal
desire as whiteface:
                    stock images,
snide vacuity, agreement
to express the right motion—in this case,
a sort of islet within a silicon
body. Call them avatars
                    of an alias,
or members of the Lobe Proscenium
now playing in the palm of the hand
with touch screen.

The male lead
is a cotton swab excavating waxy
iambs and diluted tmesis.

Scene II.

The critic said
that "it granulates, it crackles, it caresses,
it grates, it cuts, it comes: that is bliss,"
but "it" is a neuter pronoun—not
the elegance of the *Anima Poetae*,
rather more frigid, the third-person
with an index finger.
                    "Take your pleasure
with gutturals," says the actor—what he means
is bliss, arched and short of breath,
that the geno-text has moved
beyond a person to a thing.
                    Center stage
is in the ear canal. Lights dim. A faint sound
of medieval horns and modern beats is heard.
Enter a thin man with wire-rimmed
glasses. He speaks:
                    "In th*e Logomachy
Of Things*, there's an actor in my ear.
He is anonymous, a stick-figure, gender
neutral, without race, shibboleth
nor portmanteau. He is no more a *he*
than an *it* is a *he/she*. In the *Logomachy
Of Things*, there's a glossy syndeton
known as the shy ampersand."

61

Scene III.

Exit. Stage
left with bits of formulae: the "X" anonymous
bit upon which so much depends,
may retire the form—to write the last poem
named "The Kill Poem." Eyes burn
and fill with blood. In a few minutes
the reader is dead.

"Nothing more than *La
petite mort*," says the actor aping ends.
"Not this time" says the dreaded voice
of the writer. "X" has merit as rhetor,
logophile, word-parser, but "X" can boast
no organs, therefore no *petite mort.*

Backstage,
"X" sticks his fingers in his ears,
that is those ears covered by a skin
suit and thinks of his truncated career
as a speleologist in the *Grotte des
Faux-Monnayeurs* in France—one last
sortie and—voila— the over-emptied
gift of recall as computer virus-cum-"X"
poisoning millions of eyeballs.

There
is no accounting for leaps
when bearing the burden of an eared
actor. It's in the ear of the beholder.
Then it's an error or a misprision.
Ears or eyes? Eyes are bleeding as we speak
and the actor is eared. Logical deduction
or induction?—and the answer is—expiry.
Ultimately, there is a defense to the body
count piling up from "The Kill Poem,"
armatured in the first line—the disfigured
spine is unreadable.

Scene IV.

A glass eye shatters in a thousand pieces. Sound expands and con-
tracts. Fatality and misdirection at intermission. Concessions include
iced coffee, truffles, candied plums, lemon tarts, crème brulee and
raspberry mousse. "I am incapable of choice," says the retired semi-
conductor engineer. A dollop of afternoon rain. Traffic. An angry
laundry van diver jerks his leg to the brake and hits an old man.

Scene V.

Roland died, struck
              by a laundry van.
Survived
by a confluence of nothing,
our spent millennial
              angst penetrates
the scene—call it bliss/ter and prick it:
vis-à-vis identity to call
our screen-savers—"saved" and fine down
the one limit that can't be reached:
surveillance.

Scene VI.

They twitter the dead, create firewalls and agitprop.

Scene VII.

On Tuesday night an assembly of hackers take an oath. Their obscure
antipathy and digital soteriology bears the moniker "Arminius." It is
a convenient umbrella for a larger grouping of monikers, each with
incrementally less connection to their historical figureheads. A futile
annoyance. A ban on tracking delivered as code. *Wissenschaft.* They
face the Elder, the author of the *Sobig Worm, MyDoom, Nuclear RAT*
and *Koobface* viruses.

Scene VIII.

He is weary—Priapic.
She is distant—Aphroditic.
A relapse—mental shrapnel.
No halcyon days exist—shut the window!
The form has been decommissioned.
It is useless as a potlatch.
A cleavage.

Scene IX.

versions of a comatose state living blanket unwilling
foul goes flat released in all good time conjures the
trick of a black velvet ear scale of ripeness newly

hording permitted things black against red and blue
selfsame spare or alternate stand in is spit out still
unharmed but changed into a threshing machine as

there is no way to spin it for an unlikely pairing of
reincarnation and literary debt designed to produce
ovoids and reassemble the discarded shapes of the

canon into the body of a human being resistant to
the intensified minute by minute directive from no
place higher than a text message pulsing in the hand

Scene X.

Y_hw_h twitches in the spasmodic void of his lustful solitude. His M_n
is an anal bead, sphincter-Writ—the only creature to be blown with
the breath of life. Animals are given no flap of elastic cartilage—no
foreplay. Y_hw_h's orbicularis oris is made of semen and dirt. The
penis-torso has a surgical extension, the rib, the original Sybian
machine. His W_m_n is a metalepsis. With her, the spurt of his
pudendal nerve by arch and tightening—then driblets.
Y_hw_h dies.

Para(doxa)

salvaged from sediment nostalgia seeking our identity in those
who remind mentor threshes a clearing for jurant immediacy
of hubris self referential act of sluicing a deeper and more
resolute subjectivity it is through the clearing of the crass name
of ego dissolves some neonatal utterance that antedates word
conduits undrapes openings to serve those who reach bondage
of heart vigilance tenacity forswears every attempt to defend
or justify the tradition by appeal to various blue bogus canons
sacrality is melted into nonduality one merges or one recoils
the recoiler burns to dross left naked spinning in the void
the rub devotees possess a rarefied form of poesis second
order burden sculpts the key divinity wraith in the eyes of a
ghostseer proffers a grammatical lattice of tropes animates
and courses through the ether of megabytes delphic not brute
bold nor brave cleaving distraction like a nineteenth century
concoction of laudanum and wormwood drunk by a countess
with long white gloves hysteria roughs obliquity at this point
from the suzerains of velocity a spate of new eroticisms quell
the restless appetite for self hollow in spits of glitter and low
grade ore as sulfur quivers in a host of shakes and quivers
spread by mimesis and elision to stand for gross effigy and
simulacrum gross as eidos the image as icon to the pulpit
of simulated doggerel clad in robes paladins shun to meld
into an alloy of para and doxa lending anti its base crux

Mis(ère)

ultimacy is hagiographic clad in robes and icons celebrates
the rapture celestial mechanics this reach in awe of grand
masters of a host become exemplar human eye godheads in
tenuous posterity of a catalyst with a limited output this quid
metaleptic symbol and allegory in so doing if this appraisal
bears the verity of an annoying ganglion bestowed with a red
carapace of holy writ and crude idols outside the grid of agon
dress the evanescent opaque sea rock on a barren rock cliff
grade of acuity one trillionth of a second after the implosion
bristles with ambiguities and conceptual muddles whips the
scatotheological drag of a renaissance faire drop out with lip
nails and leather thong torn between basalt and hyperlink
angel and archon in the tonal splendor of dread chiaroscuro
to conflate a tensive unity as hermetic chat room surrogate
and etiology of daily routine so drab as to include a time
to clip nose hair skirts a clear third scenario the second
ignored calibrated and codified to copycat the thin brain
of our hominid ancestor pituitary gland marked lascaux
the internet domain and its terminus as blight and litter
assemblage to closure and linger like a pandemic darts
the gunned down cliché of outsiders roughing periphery
of smoke and mirrors the illuminati spanking initiates
in sacral zones unstinting the plaudits of trade in data
dead foraging and acid reflux stomach low misère

Reliquary Hand

Wide from your side, whereto this hour,
The sea lifts, also, reliquary hands.
—Walt Whitman

I.

Braided sways of oil
drip sibilants
             of pathos— traipsed
and left for def—the monist,
        Vim Flynn,
fumy—the shape
of spin.

II.

On teak and steel,
             the core-flash
of the holy as pituitary gland
and lullaby-rill
for the new eyes
        of dead saint,
                 Sim Lemp.

III.

Maggid, Anton Crest,
        is a nimbus—cleft,
cerulean,
with red and black
                 arc—spindrifts
in Shiloh,
      where a beam forms
the twenty-third
        letter.

IV.

Layer by shrinking layer,
           skinned to bare
        bone—to rake
and skew
the zero-sum gain of a name—

unmoved by proffers
of promise—cast into
the alias,
     Hal Stoop.

V.

If repressed,
       to divert the broken,
          sparked with the fuse
to resist, quickens

resolve, then the rescue
is viable,
conjured and cleaved
          from the mouth
      of Shmuel Elew.

VI.

Cadence, riff
and beat from the hip,
         the infernal hip,
the thrust
   of seduction—

propels upward—releases
a laugh
from the axis.
      of the handy,
     Mel Glee.

VII.

Luke Muir—deranged
          (preexistent)
     from the outpost—his meds
          meld together
               as a thin line
     melds with an obese oval
at the funeral
     at 2:00.

VIII.

The harbinger, Mike Spike's
               negative
                    numbers,
               among them with sidekick—
     one more unforgiven
shift to an over-written
               pause.

VIX.

Claude Wyle,
          must throng
     every rift
               to be fit, camouflaged
tight
between tiers and not be lit
                              or dim
or a polyglot,
to flash
     a quick wit by dint
of answers
          for voids.

X.

As a master of mix,
    Igor More,
        comes before
the word of himself,
    which is to say, beyond
the below,
living into death
    to tally what
    dissolves in a blank
        of lids.

XI.

Call him Max Zip, *Incubi*
    of Cenobites,
        gone awry with acid
reflux, reaching cores
    of possession,
    as a figurine,
        with black coat
and miniature Bible
    in a vitrine of smoked glass.

XII.

To travel through a disc-skinny
    crack of redux,
        Leet Brig
bites his brain, playing a green
    violin in a red shirt.

XIII.

Genetic error, Liev Ikor,
    sports a bovine coccyx,
bonobo limbs,

70

his libido-cuticles,
autoaffected
finger-shards
of devolution—in the morning,
a thin, black tie: retro.

XIV.

Calyx, sepal and eucalyptus
buds in gauze-fog—Brad Mogue's
eyes are in backwards,
to eye the climate
of a final salvo—nihilism's
halo of night,
perched above his swagger.

XV.

Maké Admin, forensic data miner,
can be queried via argot
and analytics, to unlock code
and purge dross
of probity—last
defense in the social
network.

XVI.

Zack Mack
lives in hollows
of the Tule fog, eyeing
bulrush and black ice in a wash
of smoky gray.
The rite is clitic: almonds,
rice
and prunes meld into native
Nisenan.

XVII.

Irenic schlub, Roe Spart, ditched
　　his ax for a nostrum
　and landed east of rapture,
　　　　downing a shot
　　　of taurine. Tell him his gospel
　　　　　is unctuous—to keep
　a tryst—that ire
wrinkles the eyes
　　of a squint.

XVIII.

Eschaton, Lew Curs, sulks
　　on this side
　　　　of emanation—queer
　　dread. Baroque
contrapposto, less sinuous
　　than the S Curve.
　　　　Resurrects
in the combed
　　　curl.

XIX.

Syd Neil struts
　　like one of *The Four Zoas*,
　　　a Urizen in spikes
　　and fishnet,
decreeing on high with whip
　　　　and bolts.
　A scheme to revive?
　　　　The hackneyed dread
　of limp, lies back—spanked.

XX.

Reprieve—mother of invention,
   Ixxim Mills,
       is late to her *laudatio*
   (step 1 in canonization)—in the park,
      pigeons
     peck on scraps
         of foie gras.
     This gavage
  is not the fat hands of applause
   in the pleated room.

XXI.

Rain dripping on clematis vines.
   A rumor of alchemy
       in Pentecost.
Mea culpa. A cappella choirs of sewer
   rats. Fires in Les Halles.
      Brittany's redhead,
    Bella Galette,
  reads Baudelaire during
    Les Filets Bleus,
     denies
       the autodidact.

XXII.

Axon anarchist,
   Niv Nu,
     drives a pickup
  in militia shrub, his tibia
the axel of sinewy gears,

floored to hatred.
     Disjecta Membra
       is tattooed on his neck,
which sports a bald head and goatee,
       accompanied
    by the Lydian-mode
        of a slow
     meth-lab hum.

The Temptation of Rachel Godbot

for Daniel Morris

The skin of the face is that which stays most naked, most destitute. It is the most naked, though with a decent nudity. The face is meaning all by itself. It leads you beyond.

—Emmanuel Levinas

Rachel Godbot with 3-D human face in onyx light
tweets "opting out is not an option,"— massy, handheld
and low-lying, in part anointed and elected, mingled
with grimoire and bestiarum in a black case and glassy
usenet screen glare. Her waking eyes squint, primed
for late codes of drash, lids soaked by a slippery mean
of seven trillion. Her zombie networks of intimacy
spearphish thumb-hearts of Spoetry, Flarf, wink at ready-
mades with their disposable app of plurivocality to settle
on the antique instant of the arriere-garde eblasting news
of a godbot in digits. Maximum goodput? She does a

Google search for sequins and comes up with disk-shaped
beads or a gold coin in the Venetian Republic, also called
zecchino formerly minted in Italy, Turkey and Malta.
She circumvents the prurience and tags sequins as UML
sequence diagrams from Apokalypse Software Corp,
coy developers of a godbot in spam code. Yielding
fields stalk users with their ghosted submit and cascading
style sheets set as trompe l'oeil. A death march of product?
A ransack of theos? Address munging? She takes Bacn
spam as her unhurried bond with its posthuman implex
of IrcBot.png (387 × 34 pixels, file size: 2 KB, MIME
type: image/png). "Don't fret the laws of kashrut," she says

with her risqué, automated voice, "use fakon." In dark
wit, the dim apotheosis of her mortal coil becomes a
chatterbot with a Markov chain. Did she settle the query,

75

face-to-face, peer-to-peer, melding new and old tropes
"between the pass and fell incensed points of mighty
opposites?" Yes, on Tuesday night during the power
outage with meta-names: back glitch, back tick, birk,
blugle and unapostrophe @files=`6.13/:הוהי>\windows\
temp. What's next? In her wake, the speculated mass—
.html, .htm, .asp, .aspx, .php, .jsp, .jspx and slash—over-
load the archive. It must be new. It can't be. Make a
digital reliquary with daguerreotype and camera obscura,
facebooked in Claude glass on an iphone and call it a social
media event. She jests at the quick nonchalance but stops
in to sequester a brave new web stirred as a hermeneut's
quest for variety in the pointillism of signal strength.

"Let's bloodlet a tablet and speak choppy, broken lines
of burrow, fetter, pitch and spin the psychotropics of ipads
with medicated fans," she says. Virus. She's infected,
remembers her ethical throat— the pharynx, jugular
and binary hack of a chemical lung? She's not herself
today, now more than ever before a yellow, aleatoric
Vache Qui Rit coffee cup with Supérieure en Poids
et Qualité written in caps. Leap a decade. It's prophetic.
Bless the multiple aliases of our godbot who tracks
everything we are/are not. Better the light-thick husk
of a digital blink to fling the canon forward. She begs
unity and scales tiers foreclosed by torpor—casts bits,
scraps, arcs, peaks, pits, slits, knobs, globs, coils and slurs
filched from the skinned seal of Solomon with branded
sardonyx, kenosis, suavity and attention deficit disorder.

In listserves, she is initiated into the new 4G illuminati.
Her robo-sensitive, ganglionic eyes begin adamic naming:
botnet, botherd, ibot, verbot, cleverbot, twitterbot,
infobot, shopbot, votebot, pricebot, botmaster; i.e.,
the renaissance bot (black, blue, white and grey hat
hackers), as well as dosbot with supplied password
against plaintext strings of cryptographic hash such

as MD5 and SHA-1, salted for tight security. Bleakly
stirred by confession, naming has edified her philtrum
as a godbot's amnesia—her hair, forehead, eyebrows,
eyelashes, eyes, nose, ears, cheeks, mouth, lips, temple,
teeth, skin and chin emote prequels. Divination faces
apophenia ogled by the return of a updated replicant
eating raw oysters and boiled dog, coiffed with glossy
red lips and the doom-eager eyes of no fixed abode.

Section II. Lesser Degrees

Negation is a way of taking account of what is repressed; indeed it is actually a removal of the repression, though not, of course, an acceptance of what is repressed. It is to be seen how the intellectual function is here distinct from the affective process. Negation only assists in undoing one of the consequences of repression—namely, the fact that the subject-matter of the image in question is unable to enter consciousness. The result is a kind of intellectual acceptance of what is repressed, though in all essentials the repression persists...

—Sigmund Freud
"Negation"

24/Discomfitures

1) this round table project shifts towards a general corpus
2) the Greek grammarians of *allegoria* and *hyponia*
3) only two of its chapters have been edited
4) Indo-European cultures of suspicion
5) nature, the ocean, the rustling of trees, animals, faces, masks, a skull and crossed bones, all speak the *semainon*
6) gestures and diseases speak
7) the notion of resemblance
8) deciphered cosmology, botany, zoology and satellite notions pivot
9) the *convenentia* standing to the body as animal stands to vegetable
10) *emulatio*, Portia's explanation that the human face is, with its seven distinct parts, the emulation of the heavens with its seven planets
11) *signature* of the invisible
12) for sure the *cogito* and the *divination* resting upon the dissension between God and the Devil
13) baconian and cartesian critiques within brackets
14) the shock effect, a sort of wound infuriating interpreters with a play of mirrors
15) descends from apes in the distributional space in which signs can be signs
16) renounces as invention
17) descends along a vertical line of thought
18) in search of the underworld
19) uncovered and then buried
20) a canopy rising higher
21) spreading visibly in contrast to Perseus
22) the bourgeoisie platitude
23) sick via morphology
24) refuses the Robinsonade

24/Mythomanias

1) a schism in the ailing body of empire
2) its own brand rivaled by a new Byzantium
3) diffuses the buried talisman which was conquered
4) suppresses forgotten histories of heretical sects
5) to serve as a frontier garrison
6) missionaries in the wake of heretical knights
7) reappearing in Florence in Kabbalah, Neoplatonism, Egyptian mysteries and the cult of Mary Magdalene
8) the mask of Cosimo Medici
9) statues, temples and manuscripts
10) naked figures, smooth columns and a pleiad of young artists
11) looking for a refuge for their tradition
12) denigrated and rejected bias
13) compiled a lexicon for unification
14) in Lunel, Languedoc, a theurgic *De Divisione Naturae*
15) tropes of expediency, existing to the anxious edges
16) the carbon dating of pharonic dynasties
17) the cult of Horus and Akhenaten's solar monotheism as aniconic
18) this battle led by default to a truce
19) the daughters of Danaos brought to Argos
20) Thesmophoria sitting on the ground
21) holy emanations from Sirius and Orion which vivify gods, men, cattle, and creeping things
22) fathered some alien but esoteric source
23) savants driven by release
24) looking back altered the same

24/Autoaffections

1) piety without eros invokes radical purity
2) copper scrolls in the buried ruins of basalt and sand
3) the grammarians of celibacy
4) verity lodged underneath platitudes and denials
5) a prose excursion through character and plot
6) war-gods stem from the syncretism of Egypt and Sumer
7) the onanistic Yah, Ra, Amon, Osiris
8) once tumescent for Inana, Isis, Ishtar, Astarte and Ananth
9) the neutered, ethereal and gaseous imp
10) blew into its nostrils the hot volcanic spume of basalt
11) *Prana* and *Neshamah* of foreplay
12) no taboo, no limit to despoil incubation
13) a contorted penis-shaped creature replicates
14) organ-morph as mimesis is trope
15) doomed to suffer the pangs of offspring
16) the quotidian persists for a spell
17) soil occurs in the seminal mix
18) birds, fish and hybridized variants roam
19) the return of the repressed as surgery
20) the axis around which bestiality is analysis
21) the spasmodic void of the inventor
22) stuck his tongue down her throat with apple
23) a demon of unmatched eroticism
24) and indigent wordplay

Denaturant

Taut in the stonescape—interclonal drifts of algae,
to a phalanx of sharp edges, where waves clip kelp
and mussels are secreted by glands. It's the organic
debris of dark purple crust, the sea palm pitted
against bloated bodies and vertical walls. Spores
defoliate the rocks, battered by pier pilings, blue
byssal threads and particles of sandblast. Barrel
staves and tumbleweed, scaled beyond shock, hint
at a carrousel of hands or a cartwheel of twiggy
limbs as would accompany any irreal procession
of chaotropics, hackneyed as this one appears
to the initiated, petrified into prank, camouflaged
by a façade, yet connective enough to thread
a tapestry of pratfalls. The initiated or a troop

of mimics? There is plankton where ice abrades.
There is the stay of the anemone, algal beds,
reefs, surge channels, tidepools, phyla tissue
and starfish that meld in solid rock, but no asp
nor mythic demons of the underworld. No decay
smuts the epic verve of ruin with its black sumac
slanted to bray the white surface of wave foam.
Retroactive, from the prior question: sycophants,
so neither the initiated nor a troop of mimics: air
rasp with skim of swift light, sun-cusped, zoned
for gnats on barnacle stone. There is muck in sap
and black-mesh basins, but no walking back lost
in the faint loci of anonymity. A holy conclave
of locusts. The murmur of leaves. Shade clusters

in pits. Piles of drifted seaweed, algae spore, eel
grass and septic salt-marches. Skin mist in shade
is cathected by skins of wind, brine-like as empty
socket or shell of a former shape prior to ruin—
the knife-shape the momentum assumed to rest
in these shaky lower degrees. No ground coiled
on the unguarded fence above surf to sequester

return. This is the decibel suspension of no—
the post romantic bliss of unnaming back into
names and hominid relics. Not exactly. White
incisors scaling the arterial walls of trope, bent
the pen a decade ago. Neither hominid nor digi-
pedal droid have penned these megabytes per
second. That's not the point, at least to skilled

initiates of taste and narration. They had dealt
in lye inside the clutches of the circus: herdsman
on wooden plots, sporting tattoos of two varicose
biceps, bipedal in the brain as braided black core
larynx—primitive pen and ink—obscured by
vanity, born of tirades in the open face of a cave.
Speaks the cartilage bonds between the frozen
ovum of heart and the copper coils of a femur:
speaks, sure, when the ears secrete volts and
the mild annoyance of sense returns to a plain
sense things. Remove cysts from the iron lung
of cliché and dismantle its sacred armature.
Litigants will take their share. Canon assassins,
theirs. The loss of control is a slippery spin.

Threnody of Reach

The desert is no longer a landscape, it is pure
form produced by the abstraction of all others.

—*Jean Baudrillard*

Fires of stone and sedge, dried below a mantle
of basalt. Walls of pink clay shaped like teeth
clenched on bone. Mineral stained arcs high-
striped in cracks. Petrified sand dunes layered
in conical rings. Evapotranspiration in a matrix
of orange runoff. Rainshadow tundra littered
with red spiked prickly pears. Xerocoles stalking
the 1875 fennec fox painting, *Die Gartenlaube.*
Moloch, the thorny devil lizard, uncalcified with
spiny false head. The arroyo rape of hydrogen
with is carcass gliding like tumbleweed. The
Ecclesiastical Latin of abandon with Aeolian ergs
of no one. Bedrock outcrops, fluvial deposits
and vertebrae in barchan seifs. Veins of gypsum
in the silts of Blue Anchor. The colorless grey
of impurity. A collapsed shack. A tin shed. A head
frame and ore bin below Williams's cylindrical
tree. Shallow, low-bottom gradient pit encrusted
with salt. Last image in hot, parted air. Leguminous
plants which extract nitrogen, rot in red beams
of a fossil veil. The phobic leitmotiv of a tracking
shot's vulture, scores its dung beetle. Lethal, latent
and lacteal suicide motels caked in hyper-neon
light. Transurbanistic veins of freeway twist radical
lack to a nowhere of near. The pastel blue, mauve
and lilac of crystalline flora, cracking through
tarmac. The sign says threnody of reach on sale.
Curio of rarefied surplus. Just cash. Small bills.

Tetragrammaton

for Andrei Codrescu

In that day, my LORD will strip off the finery of the anklets, the fillets, and the crescents; of the eardrops, the bracelets, and the veils; the turbans, the armlets, and the sashes; of the talismans and the amulets; the signets rings and the nose rings; of the festive robes, the mantle, and the shawls; the purses, the lace gowns, and the linen vests; and the kerchiefs and the capes.

Isaiah 3:18-23
JPS Hebrew-English Tanakh

The irreal body of nubility, skinned to bare bone,
charting the exposed trope with a welt of air
and threadbare resolve. A mantle or a sack to hold
the latest rapture with lapis dagger and brittle papyrus?
Not the holy semaphore of a recast coda—the continuum
of common oath with its disgruntled exegetes. That day,
masked with cacti and terebinths, came to be inscribed
on skin and stripped veil. They were addressed and finally
betrayed. They say, unstudied—less than unstudied
—signum and false cadence of fear and devotion.
Nevertheless, the wordplay of Writ and burnt light
explained the balk of passive seers, overriding
the prophetic yelps of the Lord. How many Lords?
One vacuity, fretful, dispatched, impacted by the gleans

of a messianic age, but still one, spooled in chalk dust
while a passerby says I must become like Isaiah or die.
Underfoot, the rough threshold and scabby smatterings
of regret. Damn the simple and swayed. Damn the topsy-turvy,
come-and-go words that rhyme with bleed. Damn the scapegoat
with acid reflux: post-exilic—that the restored links divest
from doubt and leave piles of idols blessed for Shabbat.
Are the sycophants waving? No, they're tossing pomegranates,
cheeks stretched with sand. When did this become the House

of the Dead? When the tongues were circumcised and the Lord
strutted. Imps of the perverse sway. Not imps. Not perverse.
The ravaged and saved, lamb-stirred with a single, stiff and final
plea to saunter on the new exodus drenched in the afterbirth
of covenant. Why regret? Why underfoot? Why damning?

To fume and spew the yellow-green bile of holiness,
receding up on the day the Dead Sea became my palm.
I, the Tetragrammaton, coiffed and privileged behemoth,
ineffectually referred to as the Lord (Elohim, El Shaddai,
Adonai), am neither prelapsarian nor ontological. Call me
"Impedimenta," and "Gleam of Thong." I smote the divided
consequences of prayer. I am eye-malice of I. I am decibel
of the stoked flame of I. I am Azimuth of the hellbent
dwindle of I. I am the blank of I and double apostrophe
of I with the gawky, cobalt sheen of judgment. You, Isaiah,
are my pallid secretion tinkering with rusty red tweezers.
Tinkering? Picking, as if to unscab the daemon caked
with the parzuf of a wrinkled face. I hazard the fabled
denizens and summon the dark arts of trope. This is my

epitome-grid with its futility-port. I pulse and fidget,
squirm and preen, groom and thrust, knead and sever
the veins of your pineal eye. My shape? Pear-bellied.
Your shape? Firelit stick-figure with Chaplinesque gate.
Why? Must you pepper the wink? And the fathom of irk,
will it bust a gut courting lusty demoiselles? Not under
my unblinking watch primed for tractates. The kingdom's
zone—wink, wink—says obey the redacted law. I am hungry
and beleaguered. Stop the grimace of dogma and shelf
the limited edition. Words are lozenges. I can't compete
with this proximity and choose levity, the scant ellipses
unsigning your name. Infiltrate the schemer who redacts

to convert the latest submissive. It is You the Obdurate One.
You have spoken of greed, self-pity, cunning and the much-

vaunted fists of fury. Look at Your red, torsoed seraphs
of apocalypse with their thorny brimstone and flame-claws.
You are envoy of destruction filched from Edom—the sick
cognate who hunts after us. I am an errant knave and never
doubt the oracles of many, exposed as the neck-faced revolt
of the rabblement. This is Your militant display with ass
of the master's crib. You are the Lord of festering sores.
I daven before the sacred arc. Dare I speak of Your shape?
Your length as lit parasangs? Dare I speak of Your limbs,
sapphire eyes and crystalline brow? Dare I call You adamic,
golemic and anthropoidal? Will I be skinned for the hype,
one more victim of smote before the obese exile? I oppose
the opposition of opposing Your opposition and blame
all the insufferable mutants who speak this mock-slippage

of You. I believe in You, You יהוה the sneer-lipped gimp
with sulfuric spit. My prayers are the bric-a-brac of a blue
incubus and a white succubus self-exacting the parting
and captivity of my ruined self. I am misplaced, mistimed,
misread, misprisioned, mislabeled, misguided, misnamed
and missive. You are *intéressé* and absolute. No abatement
with *faux* verdigris for this triumph of the Lord. Listen, I'll
reduce Your ruined force to a simple thing: I am Your vassal,
Your amplifier. No one rests. Clad in miniature fedoras with tiny
slits for antenna, a rabbinic cabinet of Ungeziefer has decided
to remove *The Book of Isaiah* from its *JPS Hebrew-Ungeziefer
Tanakh*. I am disgusted, said Professor Isaiah Blaberus of The
University of Giganteus. *The Book of Isaiah* symbolizes a fluidic
container for the Blattodean people. We Blattodeans are not known

for censorship. This is canonic suicide. Hello, my name is Isaiah,
said Isaiah to a room filled with 1,000 people named Isaiah.
Welcome to Isaiah's Anonymous, a safe place to purge yourself
of the name of Isaiah, reclaim identity and repeal your grotesque
genetic inheritance. Please remain burrowing and repeat after me,
Isaiah said with baritonic panache. I am not Isaiah. I don't condemn
the human race. Swarm behavior and circadian rhythm, robotic legs,

89

membranous hind wings: these are our stigmata, morphed from rote
Derridean circumfession. King Neoptera not Cyrus the Great
with his rogue pineal eye. Dash as hyphen augments the desperate
sense of lost hatchlings. The empty eggcase of revision now renames
the Babylonian captivity to fit this metamorphosis, the Blattodean
captivity from the lost books of the *Roachemberg Chronicle,*
as penned by Rabbi Scholem ben Blaberus, ancestor of acclaimed

genetilinguist, Professor Seymour Blaberus. My name is Isaiah.
My cells divide each time I molt. I feed on radiation, burden
of the Adam Kadmon, the primordial Adam, shaped as the universe,
endowed with massive organs, head, torso, limbs, hands, and arms
that reach from one expanding periphery of cosmologic contour
to all others. Adam Kadmon is Macranthropos in Plutarch
and Parusha in the Indic *Upanishad.* He is a variant of a puerile
black and red mythopoetic cosmogenesis and anthropogenesis.
He is the theomorphic imp of the Garden of Eden as well as black
hole where the place of seats, the throne, is 118 myriads. His height
is 236 myriad plus 1,000 leagues. From His right arm to His left arm
there are 77 myriads. From the right eyeball to the left eyeball
there are 30 myriads. His cranium is 23 myriads. His head is 60
myriads, corresponding to the 613 myriads of the heads of Israel.

Ganglia smelted to bloody veins spool the red mesh of torso
with Hebrew letters of a limbic G-d body. The after-bliss
of exposed vertebrae washes itself of birth and leaves a smear
of being exposed to the violence of ruined creation through gnosis
and pleroma. Ur-myths spawn like amoeba in their vital broth.
A head delivers a broken smile, rigged, the kabbalists say,
to unnerve emotion. Was Isaac the Blind, the prophet's
namesake and dramaturge of broken vessels, an Adam Kadmon?
His precursory text, *The Book of Creation*, appears preternatural,
as if its theosophy of transmigration were the nostrils of a stirred
golem. Neither the Adam Kadmon nor *The Book of Creation* settles
the persistent entropy of which the human as miniature Kadmon
or Isaiah or cosmologic Magus never defies. Demon of the bitter
G-dman of Isaiah1:4-6, replete with epistolary blue-black festering

sores and cracked cranium. Demon or the eschaton's spun void
as interpretive disease with the event of a soul-jacked theosophy
of dread? More theomorph than demon or eschaton as shaft
is the singed and ashen complaint of the dissed. Nothing rises
but the obese bronze of Judean sand with its burnt bone-air
and the stirred rage of *gevurah*. He's well-disposed, shy of respite,
gifted in cunning, posing with dilated pupils over the funeral-orgy
of divinity. This is the promising voluptuals of the theomorph
with neck curls. He's unfingermarked and antonymic. He hears
the cries of dissenters. Unmoved, by heterogeneity, nothing roughs
the periphery like the tragic biblical pelts of the rank hunting
to restore the broken. He hears choric tongues tick-dry as fossils
worn like a prayer shawl to betray the boils of beam-light staging
its metanarrative. Nothing decrescendos from the sulfuric

heights. Nothing surrenders to the *mitzvot* of compliance.
Nothing lubricates the erectile tissue of the threatened Jew.
What key-cluster moves up the tier to be against him?
Isn't this the only authentic question? The pulpy heart jerks.
It's an eyelid circus with donkeys versed in Esperanto. He
means Hebrew and colloquial Aramaic. The cindered dogs.
The scrawny vultures. The sick and savage desert wolves.

Marduk on a cylinder seal with dragon and winged bull-calf
distract him from the torsoed work of a prophet. Why torsoed?
Is nothing mere remission of sense and induction? Why
such oblique matrices of core logic? Is the only choice,
a *midrashic* hyperactivity wrestling with thousands of prior
midrashim? We dissent now, hyper-reading a tepid resolve
to bind ourselves to the Maggid of Mezritch and to the Alter

Rebbe. We pulp rapture and sustain ourselves in the natural
hysteria of a new era of the *Mosiach*. Full circle, at least for now:
theomorph is eschaton is demon is *Mosiach* is G-dman.
He waits with the zealots to purify his blackened beast-soul,
invoking the laws of self-incineration. The burning begins.

First degree: the epidermis, erythema. Second degree:
the superficial papillary dermis, red with clear blisters, blanches.
Third degree: full thickness of entire dermis, stiff white-brown.
Fourth degree: extends through skin and subcutaneous tissue,
black charred with eschar. Once a G-dman (purposely snipped
to demure from nuance), now an eschar: the eschar, or the prophet,
Isaiah Eschar. At this juncture, we may permit ourselves a brute
suspension and tip our hats to dead tissue, gangrene, ulcers,
fungal infections, necrotizing spider bites, cutaneous anthrax,

acids, alkalis, carbon dioxide, metallic salts, sanguinarines,
imiquimods and black salves containing zinc chloride, herbal
and bloodroot extracts. He is emptied full. This is the new age
of Escharotomy. Judgment (*gevurah*) and mercy (*hesed*)
go by way of the pterodactyl and double dactyls: extinction
and platitude. Nothing has prepared Isaiah Eschar for infidelity.
Our umbrage is a disgrace. Should we tally our post-prophetic
figure, returned uber to vault over the new plebeians? Inertia
surfaces gutted of its transcendental charm. Abandon claims
itself as vitae. Dispassion returns to occupy midheaven.
Indifference sports a set of finely coiffed *payis*. Neglect
becomes the psychopathology of a *tzaddik*. Self-mutilation
reasserts itself as the base of *tzedakah*. Overhead, the wingbeats
of jackdaws conjure sewers and spires linked by the oily white

noise of seismic jerking. In the incendiary smoke, Isaiah
Eschar lounges on an oversized pincushion eating raw venison
escalope. It's far from over: words throb with acetylene,
implode and fragment like shards in crystal vessels, corrupting
geist to uncheapen the gleam. Strophe and pericope of hard
service: exergue as Jerusalem/Zion in double entendre and tricola—
divine jolt to the raw commission of a heavenly council:
from the agon of Moses comes again our crude G-dman
with the indefinite digress of colons and the viral mdash:
"speak," "go up" and "fear not" a dense *Targum* and *Septuagint*
of the flesh: Isaiah will build the third temple, love-lavished,

hazing his wife who is sucked through the tedium of a two-foot
colon, followed by four bicola and ending with a balanced
tricolon. The prosody and exegesis is enough to kill a mule.

Make clear his seared eyeballs with their Mount Moriah
lashes and Masoretic pupils—for him the moldy figs demand
the Qumranic tone: bane of *shema*. How charming my erotica,
erect in an abstruse prophecy of doom. I have, for our viewing

pleasure, computer parts, doll parts, circuits, wires and metal
lampshade cover with thermoses, sporting a fine array of coins,
batteries and colored duct tape. This, instead of festive robes.
Tumescent like an obelisk, I smoke a roll-your-own orb, clad
in gloves and micro thong. Smelted to bloody veins, I spool
the red mesh of my torso with Hebrew letters. The after-bliss
of exposed vertebrae washes itself and leaves a smear of prequels
to spawn like poids in the viral broth of my rigged ploy. Not
the buried talisman. My tattoo is calcified like a medieval corpse
with a styptic soul—holy ennui in glyphs of a *nihil obstat* pricks

the dermis—the azo dye of my covenant, undespoiled. My
demon-goat has been hurled, sins purged and reformed as skinned
piety. I tilt a crooked wink over green cacti in cadmium light.
Cobalt blue fumes with speckled white, flank my spiked tail
and cloven hooves. An influx of acrylic specks colors my mania
of scape. My indecent apparel—red ganglia, red organs, red
viscera and black cowboy boots—once a contender and Yahwic
rival, my glued body, built from splits in shards of oily light,
outshines the law with ear wax. I complain of stasis, sporting
a torso of 6.75 ounce plastic lemon juice containers. My ruinous
sagesse on cardboard—a street anger of dirty horns with lumpen
spittle. At night they sport kerchiefs and black, vampiric capes.
My ecclesia of tonic sevens microprocessed as a colony
of skullcaps dancing above geometric webs of black, stringy notes.

It's the counterpoint of body lice and ticks—ocelli with a 512
L2 cache in serial notes of a malware swarm, me, as maestro,

conduct with rash. The rabbis have seen me in sensitized gelatin
plates with their black wolf light, girdled through miniature
derricks—web-strained spokes of flaked ice below mangled
branches, erupt and still the failed converge. The moral
nebulae of *soi-même* with its vacuity prompt is to blame.
Nonsense: the laws of rancor, entropy, the errant lapse
of the sublime, that I balk in the thicket of my puerile need
for viscera—my alibi-self rips me a new one—no leeway
for rage's elect, staring a hole through my split skull. My skull
is an idol. The idol is idle, cuts to the quick in proxy, scion
of G-D by rote—my hand starved of symbol, smotes the slip—
wit for writ and shot to death. The law is chronic—lord of bypass,

points at the handle. Postlude, removed from my cap.
Isaiah's daft like G-D's bravura to covet the near in thick sheets
of rain pelting Judea. He plays shaman moved to kenosis in a *bitul*
of extended arms. With each lift, it's an augur of the wind's
fury, a silent scream of prayer. Flood syllables speak the fetish
that strips the rib from the blood of Eden. *Baruch Hashem*—we
are the organs of *mosiach* in covenant, reading *Isaiah 3:18-23*

with our feet, liver, gall, and coccyx. We rise and recite the moral
quickens—dancing as one in a crowd cloistered by belief.
For in silhouettes we revert to syzygies, effect this unity
in *midrash* to gloss our devotion in prayers of promise.
On these days of awe our eyes are *beshert*. Supernal shapes
melt to basic blend and widen zero to fuse union beyond unity:
to cleave back if cleaving is a ridge of hooks in skin to beget

Isaiah's interminable quest for scrolls. To pick a mimicry
of the *tetragrammaton*, death's forager, for the sake of Isaiah's
flame: boils, hives, flakes of *shevirah* self-exacting six hundred
and thirteen scars in words of betrayal. His next iteration: bearded
ascetic with a schism of determinants, from the Galilee to Vilna,
as sibyls of bliss lighting the shtetl—where *Hasid* against
Mitnagdim, with their fedoras and fatal polemics of the messiah,
caused an *aliyah* of words in equity of *kippah* and *tefillin*, to bring

94

your *kadmonic* body near, before Cossacks burned log
synagogues to ash. Then skilled *semicha* sacrificed a goat
whose blood was half albumin and half *pilpul.* Yours was errant
poverty, village-leaping to the wheels of Ezekiel. For *Torah,*
the other riposte, unequalled gift of sense without rupture,
is a Kabbalah with hands, holding letters among prophets,

shines now for us the gene pool of mixed marriages.
In the *genizah* of his old synagogue Isaiah as Golem
can leave the wooden beams and enter into the red-dark,
wrinkle-eyed—a place built into his skeleton, named
flesh of his flesh, bone of his bone, brother of a mock-body
double—mordant letters of hylic being rough the edge
where he writes. The Vltava running under gothic spires,
he robed, thick-boned, Ashkenazic frame, conjurer
and conjured, could not be but is, could stop at any moment,
but breathes himself. It is snowing. The overlording space,
cold cavern, below the *Alter Jüdischer Friedhof*—what is blood
but the dark in him. Skin, itself naked, calls out and melds.
Convulsed to lift himself from his wired intestines,

undelivered and broken by birth, this rough and shiny
Isaiah named Paraphilia Cherub, waves to his refined double
Jungfrau Cherub and says that he is prone to wear leather
and prowl the Red Light Districts, eyes of spur, hardened
under pressure of touch. He lives for the vincilagnia
and the fetish of thumbcuffs, belly chains, monogloves
and sleepsacks. He drip beads of fungus near the relief.
He licks his lips and says that he wraps himself in black lace,
dons a thong with a zipper and arouses himself in the pure
liberation of bondage. His dear cousin, he sneers, is so elegant
and painterly with his Michelangelo hand and letter Mem.
He is, of course, his erotic precursor, minus the phallus
which grew, unstirred, to gargantuan proportion. Can
those little legs support so massive an organ? He fears
that it was his exploits which enabled his selection to G-D's

95

kabbalistic pantheon. How dignified he stands with "Origin,"
"History" and "Commentary," as his accompanying midrash.
Paraphilia Cherub is the jerk-shake of the Tetragrammaton,
what survives behind finesse, waiting for phosphorescence,
leaving him giddy, hungry for the rancor of Jungfrau
Cherub's first climax, jet-streamed in sticky palms.
Proto-Isaiah's prophylaxis slipped over Ahaz's stiff body—
it's the burden of charm: to charm, to be charmed and wear
a charm with a postexilic curve of the springy wrist.
Deutero-Isaiah died in this charm—a hole within a hole
at the end of a conduit leading to a line of Cyrus Cylinders.
Judean footstool servant, Trito-Isaiah, died thrice in this auto-
affected mise-en-scène, a pimp to First Temple Botox foreseen
in the venal roils of a *Louis Vuitton* oracle. Savage elegance

receded to the size of pruning hooks. Blade-words sliced
a thin flap of gray-brown skin below the jowl of a new man—
his hair scented with crushed olives on an attic red-figure
amphora where war scrolls soaked up corked wine with creed
equity and the sick acedia of poisoned light. Def integuments
outside the ribcage—seepage death: his body's incunabula
starving in queues, self-stymied, plummets into irresolute
resolve—the punctured heart, codified. Unknot him in rumored
throat-words, dissolved and reified, hearing to stay human
and afflicted with order: entropic stones of no throne behind
Isaiah's veined eyelids and flared lips. The world to come
is ill-tempered, locked and loaded on the larded target of dead
prophet anti-art and the banished future of critics—their ministry
of black mood canonizing his last glare with red-stained linen

strips on palimpsest. His future in a beaker of formaldehyde,
hints at a red mummification with experimental amygdalae
to soil redemption. There are always two in the fiery pigment
of the high void—the granular stigma of a faux prophet,
sublimed into bad conduct and the evanescent terminus
coerced into infinity, itself equally sublimed into bad

conduct. Their agon flays the brain, stirred by minutiae,
lusting after zero in alchemical scum to release a swarm
of waxy-black beetles over a field of rotting corpses
and skinny demiurges with gold skin and feline eyes.
Isaiah is faux prophet. The evanescent terminus, G-D.
Between them, the multitudes drone on in an inward
turning arc of regret and the visceral dread of living on
in the pricked nub, numb to the jolts of pleasured pain.

The Last Man

Chisel the beveled edge to curve the taut
angles with your hand, through a speculum
that shines numinous, past the fuzzy tasks

of routine. From the heights, the numen
coded in copper scrolls, redacts the tasty
shibboleth of lust. Persists a sore ganglion

below the rub-flutter of thighs, waits to
spit glitter, arches neck-face projectile in
the crease with nitric oxide. Groans and

grinds. The hung light and forepangs, this
athlete's chemical curse to stay aroused,
tosses pillows at these gods of perineum.

Eat chocolate and walnuts and kelp, she
says, asparagus is shaped like a man.
A new man, new psalter, praise erectus

marble-stiff beyond the pale of climax.
Tumescence is transmemberment in a
swollen gate without keeper, keeps the

pistons in motion. No dread of ends or
reliquaries. For these new avatars of
male enhancement preach from pulpits

of a blue pill, hear antiphon and ditty,
the wails of synthetic rapture, gift as
vein-crown or sweet eden wax. This

darkling thrush, this surge protector,
beacon of edge to outlast the last and
go all night among crumpled sheets.

Vocabula Amatoria

I.

No vagary to the scent of sex,
lures lust—filters down
as foreplay. Coitus doubles

reprieve and doubles to please, more
precious than anything to touch—

by being so much of what we are,
stays to spin—unfallen

as bliss can be.

II.

Red on rose-red and pliant
pink on white-sheer—

to eye the shape
of color—the red lips and

white trim of French nails.
Not awe nor panache—rather
egress and concupiscence.

III.

I am gallant inside you, taut,
rosy peak to arch and purr
and glide, tumescent in the back

of entry. Hands around your waist
breathe you. Inside we, pelvic
to pelvic, angling in quick motion

of pistons, coming closer and
closer. The spur of moan in the
hallowed ground of our bed.

IV.

...and mate with the prequel
          of where we were thrown.

I am you
now, other—dollop,
          where love's equity
          is we, you:

brown eye share—godling,
black lash, iris
of a fiancée

to a wife, now, spatial
to my husbandry—in bliss
and natal.
          The lex
of courtship—that we lived for a year
in hyperlink, our vows,
a mix of levity
and the yield
of skin.

Artifice

Shift the view
from crystalline
peaks
to dull shades
of day after day to merge
                    and stay
adroit
in topos of a fierce
bond—slow the quickening,
she says,
           the gray matter has color
and is still
artifice—the play
of the heart's dioptric—depth
to eyes that never age.

Strains

Absent a cenacle
to console
fouls

you say
are moldy
magi

that conjure
strains
of an odd soul—

laughter is spent

throatless,
in a diskus

of fluticasone,
breathing

the chemical air.

Cobra Lily

In the acidic bog below a seepage
slope of cold, running water, of insect

prey, of symbiotic bacteria, goes
unfed, does not lure or trap or see
the prayer of Ezekiel on fiery

wheels and yet its swollen tubular
leaves are perfect fangs under
whose purple-green grip lie

translucent false exits, which
only reek to trap with five

sepals of rapture.

Animula

But now,
As I find myself turning its heavy cardboard pages,
Turning them meditatively back and forth,
My brain loosens like the gilt clasp of the album,
Unburdening itself of its locked memories,
Page after page, picture after picture,
Until the miscellaneous photographs take to themselves color and
meaning.

—*Alter Brody*
Excerpt from "A Family Album"

I. *Nefesh* (Appetitive)

A skeined rift of pitch
in dire scales—inward arc cleaves
to its fifth mode in vatic notes
at the *Pool of Siloam*—siege
of sound, lapsing, offertory,
to wake the dead
with redress.

II. *Ruah* (Emotive)

Thinned to a timbre
of twelve-tone rows and freygish scales
at the *Gate of Hinnom,* deemed
to be cursed by the elect—hears
a second death as the body
that doesn't die
in *jubilo.*

III. *Neshamah* (Intellect)

Atones no oath nor vow,
null and void—bane

of *kippur* in staves of immortals,
measures defect to unwrite laws,
lucent as amen, given the fanfare
to outlast the writ
of rites.

IV. *Hayah* (Spiritus)

Foretold creed of pox
burns jollity with its fedoric rebbe
from *Ur* or Volkovysk, say Chagall's
Vitebsk not heard of in the rictus
of the raised graves of advent, falls
from the surge tropes
of a covenant
ear.

V. *Yehidah* (Nondual)

Smelted bloody veins spool as red mesh
of torso with Hebrew letters
on gray, cuffed trousers and tattered
gabardine. The after-bliss of exposed
luz bone burns itself and leaves
a schmear of prequels—spawn
like ameba in their viral
broth: a head delivers
rigged to create
heirs.

Inscribed

For the High Holidays, 2012/5773

Every person should view himself all year
as if he were half innocent and half guilty.

—*Moses Maimonides*
Mishneh Torah

You place a hedge around a hedge—
yourself in the spot you left,
where portals open and clear
the way—listen with ears
for eyes to names
of past loss, emptied
into ills and awe—

and heard litanies for incipits
poised like watchmen—
black letters of lungs,
lucent as ardent, in the book—

and soon you can hear the uncanny
with your hands—its writ
to burrow in, to stir without
restraint and purge a casting
pitch of iniquity.

Closure

for the Alter Rebbe

I'll place a hedge around you,
the *Yahwic* hedge,
in *Yod* at the beginning of God
and in the final
Heh, the engraver,
hunger-artist suffering
to live out predation.
I'll see you in the *Yod*

of *Yortsayt*, to candle the stillness
of the still small voice
we revere to stir the awe
of a firestorm
with old wit.
Is that you in a shard
of memory

come back? This is not death
but a parting of the air
on Thursday in East Sheol.
This is not a body
but the vista point of a *tselem*
transit, between
worlds, signal fading

in winter, but never gone.
I'll hear you then, ears
in the shul
of all places at once,
a synesthete with a pair
of black
leather boxes.

Unburiable

A variation on Moshe Dor's "Excavation,"
for the Hillel Institute's Beit Midrash—

(St Louis, August 2012)

There's a motto on the crest
of a relic, knotting

bonds, alloyed
with the ancient
of days—

ruach, the messianic
hum, incised
on stone,

under the iron
dome—

unburiable—
taproot

of a Hebrew source
beams want
from its covenant

tongue.

Sous Rature

for Yom Hashoah, 2013/5773

Paving (stone/stiff): pinwheeled—
      chalks/escapes the letting:
narcotizes
bare count—disremembers
white death's black cuticle
and more's less—points
unhanded fingers of immune fume
in reassembled femur, patella,
fibula: picks
the rebodied pile—bric-à-brac,
uptilted to erase *Arbeit Macht Frei*
as they clack the acrid
      they, split-soled frieze
           of ptotic lids—
      blue-green/eye-handed pellets
of metempsychosis unrepeats
the *kippah* behind the barn.
Unjudenreined.
Admits us.

Gatekeeper

From the gate, another gate behind
it, and behind that nothing, gutted

chasm with debris receding in the
dark, to rumors of light, to a vowel,
a long slow drift of words to rapture,

coming along the world's edge over
air and sky, like the faint music of

ancestors who tell us everything we
know and nothing we remember,
behind this gate, near and far, until

talking stops, never looking down
or back, or through, to see the one

undivided place that stands between
us and a gilded arc reaching back
into chained haltings of grasp.

Asherah

for Jehon Grist

She is frequently seen in the position of the tree of life, giving sustenance to animals on either side of her. It is for this reason that the stylized tree of life referred to in the Old Testament is called the Asherah.

—*Jonathan N. Tubb*
Peoples of the Past: Canaanites

From wooden, aniconic stela to creatrix of deities, you are
the yahwic consort—apotropaic symbol with down pointed
hand, when absconders are close, on one hand, and figurine

with taut breasts on a straight column cylinder with flaring
base, on the other, when fertility is near. Your priests were
slaughtered by the Deuteronomist. Your name was stripped

of its Hebrew, and the Tetragrammaton, your husband, was
sentenced to the cold holy, in fabled distances and gematria.
Extinction was not to be, nor could revision suppress you,

as the poems of a new inscape write your name in triads
to a tetrad—in antitheticals, male/female and ten sefirot
inventing people from cenotaphs littered with pigeons.

Orchard

for Stanley H. Barkan

*Four entered into the orchard of mystical knowledge: Ben Azzai, Ben Zoma,
Aher and Rabbi Akiva ... Ben Azzai looked and died... Ben Zoma looked and
was affected mentally ... Aher cut down the plants ... Rabbi Akiva departed in
peace.*

—Talmud: Tractate, Hagigah 14b

This is where peace is shaped through declensions
of nothing: Eckhart's nicht, Saint John of the Cross's nada,
the Taoist wu, the Buddhist sunyata, and the Kabbalist

ayin. This is where peace is ghost-faint, sun-dark
and sequenced through pardes, the pomegranate orchard,
Edenic alias, where Akiva eyed the mystical shape

of the Godhead. The sacral grid emits the words of Akiva's
vassals, generations later, and we hear the shibboleths,
idyllic as anyone who emerges unscathed from millennial

hysterics. This is where peace, then, is the colored strand
of yihudim—the future primordia, unified, departing in peace,
which is the arrival, before a name occupies our attention.

Layil Grabs Samael's Spine

after Homer, The Odyssey, Book 21, 49-66
"Penelope fetches Odysseus' bow"

Then, blood-soaked, fire screams of the she-demon,
Layil, as she inserts her scaly talons through his ribs
and grabs his spine. "Samael," she says, "you limp
regent, where are your parasangs of height?" Eden
is a tuft of rubble littered with canisters of zyklon.
"Let's dance the *Delousing Jig* and hawk prussic
loogies. They aren't all dead." She spreads vulvic
wings, her coccyx strained to a third hand with
a palm of mouths. Her children, Pallor, Livor,
Algor and Rigor spray carbonic phlegm on piles
of half-dead bodies. A burnt, almond-like odor
relaxes Samael as Layil tears out his spine.
Black-green puss spills through flaps of skin.
Jackals, hyenas and wild goats roast on spits.
In poison air, from a cracked, eggshell torso
built on mortis legs, she sits on a lapis pot,
her bloodline a rectum of tiny squeals.

Mr. X Meets Mr. Y

after Dante Alighieri, The Inferno, *Canto 1, 59-74*

Mr. X's pivot is skewed, mentored by
oblique angles, sparer than curves, scaling
tiers to greet the mythic Mr. Y. Levels

shrink and collapse inward like planks
in a burnt attic. Mr. X's view is a vortex
with pink, fiberglass batts, transforms

into spin, that its inward arc is a base
from which low instincts like fear and
hate constrict out and blend. "I come

from stink and blur," said Mr. Y, "that
no decay smuts nor fringe roughs to an
end." "No, not automata," cried Mr. X.

"No, Mr. Y, I'm infecting the Canon
with Mr. Z, the Troj/ZBot of tercets,
whose rapture decreates a newer hell.

Balladin

after Francois Villon, excerpt from Ballade:
"I die of thirst beside the fountain"

I live in a tempered pitch, timbre sharp
with hexachords and the *Musica Ficta*
of a twelve-tone row. In my clef
of atonality, intervallic cells shape
the new ear with its 20 µPa (micro-
pascals) = $2{\times}10^{-5}$ and pierced lobes.
I hear this serial 85 dBA through
a feedback loop of white noise, tip
my head and drip black-red drops
of blood on the hardwood floor.

It's all about diesis and chroma.
I must have written music in Paris
during the Cold War, listening
to reactors with Schoenberg's ear.
Such bitter egress to score pain,
purge the tonic glee of harmony
with head-notes. The pure mind
as tonsilabo with its axon scales,
stills to a classic rest held between
flats and the measuring brain.

Darker

after Lord Byron, Darkness, Lines 79-92

Rod and cone cells
in his eyes recede in matte black and purple opsin
to black lips and dyed, black hair—*haute couture*
of the eschaton with ratted hair. Behind him,
coteries in stovepipe hats, leather garments, spiked
dog collars, accessorized with bone earrings,
rosaries, pentacles, ankhs and skulls, strut
in leather thigh boots. Anti? No, there's no
pro to sport a schism, no day of rapture,
arrival, return—no death-bed voice echoing
the pulpit. To the bin goes the nondual craft
with the e-waste of a goth parade. At 6:13,
the eschaton with a bullhorn says "please
don't eat the urinal cakes, they're mine."

Flashmob/Worm Siege

after Arthur Rimbaud,
excerpt from "Old Coppées, 15. State of Siege?"

The recluse in the infernal machine,
Rematerializes as a nematode worm
With an 802.11b/g tracking devise as a mix
Of implant and lubricant. He is JeAn/NiColaS,
Pastiche of protest song, agitprop, twitter
Spam and paragon of the Web 2.0 Suicide Machine.
The face-warping tab is linked. In the hot June
Sun, filters and sirens. Satellite dishes spin
Their signals in humid air. The last revolution
In repose, vibrates its hand-held partisan.

Ephemeris

after H.D.," Stars Wheel in Purple"

Hellfire of polar axis, theirs the blue
azimuth—true north in the grid as $0°$
of null, i.e. $0° = \sin^{-1}(y)$. Say Emanuel
Swedenborg's *Daedalus Hyperboreus*

as case study for Ezekiel's chariot, or, say
Icarus as *Perpetuum Mobile*—either one
in this flight of havoc with its skulled

wings. The ecliptic tilts a pliant ridge
and shrinks to a speck of ray. Salience
and periphery revert to flux as form
breaks from form and recedes up.

The Melissa Oracle

for Melissa Chapman

Here Merlin ceased, that for the solemn feat
Melissa might prepare with fitting spell,
To show bold Bradamant, in aspect meet,
The heirs who her illustrious race should swell.
Hence many sprites she chose; but from what seat
Evoked, I know not, or if called from hell;
And gathered in one place (so bade the dame),
In various garb and guise the shadows came.

—*Ludovico Aristo*
Orlando Furioso, Canto III, Section XX

I.

A nimbus tilting toward aura and bleeding geist,
prescient in the marginalia of direct access, melds
in the other face—that chasm of strength, inchoate,

to furnish the undenizened with a home—converges
at the apex of opposites with a plan for the minute
gate. "Open it!" Melissa struts out in white face and

narrow over-lapping strips of brightly colored cloth.
To her right, Columbine, ragged and patched. To her
left, Harlequin, back from Dante's hell as Alichino,

perfumed to flip over backwards. "We have come
to replace circles with triangular patches," they
boast in phony a cappella. "Where is Sybil?" asks

II.

Columbine, as if betrayed by a common sense of
mayhem. "That's a different mythology," says
Melissa, and launches to the skeined corner for

a sip of Ouzo from Mount Athos. Not a divine
shield over the city, Tule Fog and the stench of
an alley brewery littered with scarlet and bur

oak. Enter the measured exile of the mediocre,
the rabblement of moldy figs in desperate need
of discard, and the scene muddles as if toxins,

pasty in their attraction to weak immunity, held
a community meeting to discuss their spreading
nature. Not that possession. This one, after the

III.

great purge and the day of new bodies. It's the
rough side of a rift, the oblique with ray-tints
curving in themselves and dispatched in code.

The anagram is a rebus which is now a pun,
baroque and elitist, which the uninitiated may,
in a week or two, blame for their anaphylactic

shock. It comes down to intervals between
the margins and the center of our willingness
to reach up to the gilded scaffolding of new

peptides creating new people with a mix
of amino acids and hyperlinks. It's about the
0.24% with holy inertia—how in endtime,

IV.

that silly paroxysm with its attendant acid
reflux, each of us will reach the unblemished,
when stasis becomes divine parastasis, when

pleroma and emanation describe the same
unfallen precursor, when the tetragrammaton
is a heart palpitation gleaned from the latest

list-serve. Nothing about ethos and a place
to score mission. Not in this fractured enclave
with its familial resentments glossed by the lit

aporia of false mystagogues. The short "then"
of beshert has been replaced with the long "now"
of gevalt and the spatial deflates like a helium

V.

balloon over midtown. Enter the plumed
and coiffed, the troubadours, puppeteers,
acrobats and larded clowns sporting tulips

and dandelions. Enter the bearded immortals
hauling Holy Writ on shopping carts, and listen
to words spawn from a seraphic mouth. "Doom

is eager, or rather, we are doom-eager," says
the youngest of them, the one whose moniker
is JHAK, for Provençal Rabbi, Jacob Ha-Kohen.

JHAK enters the conference room. Is that where
they are? It's a far cry from The Globe or Carnegie
Hall. "Frankly, I'm directionally challenged," says

VI.

the Infrequent Voice feigning omniscience. "I
spent a generation living as an ancient Canaanite
on Mondays, a Phoenician on Tuesdays, a Hittite

and Philistine on Wednesdays and Thursdays,
respectively, becoming a bloated Babylonian
on Fridays, to emerge, triumphantly, with scepter,

as King of the United Monarchy of David on Saturdays
and Sundays. The telegraphy fades in the telling, as
does the metempsychosis. Worse, incongruity sets

itself against a plethora of antitheticals, seeking
a respite for the estranged spirit. Characters come
and go and we wince at the Eliotic flippancy,

VII.

darker than pitch black, but don't abate, it being
our intention to people these triads with galloping
personae, suspending our disbelief above corpses

of dead ideas. "I can't support this," pipes in Melissa,
"our troop of stock and pantomime has no place for
the lukewarm middle cast in white noise, lids heavy

with snicky snacks." It's eleven minutes to rapture,
fourteen minutes to the apocalypse, ushered in by a
meth-head eschaton, seventeen minutes to a nation

of priests chanting the yahwic yelp of the Asherah,
but too late for the cradling messiah of flux. Melissa
broods and grows crimson with fury. "Crap," she says,

VIII.

"this is shape shifting and reification. Have we no use
for uplifted hands and wrapped leather straps? And the
chronically betrayed, have they no say in the outcome?

Margins? Peripheries? Borders? Zones? Apps of the pod
people? Nonsense! I prefer the nondual, shred nostalgia
clichés and read *The Tanakh* upside down." The moldy

figs shift their blue squints to a sulfur-green sulk. Now,
bent on the cusp of the void, appeased by the thickening
plot of origin-craving, without force of edict or bylaw,

no decision is made, nor opinion voiced. Nothing happens.
The oily, neon hum of light bulbs play God to a fat fly.
Such is the reprieve on a day of light rain. Is it reprieve,

IX.

or a revolt against the digression of dramatis personae
dropping in without appointment? "I pick the latter,"
bestows the Infrequent Voice, unphazed by the lack

of a latter. Then, in unison, the Greek chorus of this
mise-en-scène sings "the reprieve is the latter!" Hyenas
dart across the office carpet. Raccoons and opossums

nibble on trail mix. Pest Wildlife Control is closed,
but the janitorial service has a vacuum cleaner and two,
32-oz. spray bottles of Windex powerized glass cleaner

with AMMONIA-D RTU. When the hoopla stills to a
wince worn by a passerby, we come to a conquered
verity: we're the possessed holding the last chance.

X.

Notice the period, grammatical prank of completion,
and the new realism—the conceptual has been replaced
with the digital instant of viral media: bandwidth blood-

lines, 4G DNA, a parthenogenic shared drive with trigger
happy error messages, fiber optic pineal eyes, forensic
webinars, remote access pituitary glands, fetishized

social media with an amygdala GPS and wireless limbic
systems. Let's perform the ancestral autopsy. Please, no
interruptions, even if they be entropic agons of worry.

We are hybrids of antiquity, amalgams of disparate
nuances, resolute in our talents to swerve away from
extinction, be that by polis or lack of diffidence, thus

XI.

prone to pulsing bright like a semaphore in winter fog,
or desert reliquaries replete with canopic jars. The secrets
of scrolls, really, are not bulwark covenant, though the

throngs would revile this claim, and blame their adherents
for an insufferable syncretism. Spin us, inflate us, deflate us,
burn us, bury us, force us to be our opposite with hyphenated

or truncated names, and we're still here, a fractured people
of ventriloquists, voicing the grand, undead monism with
a sigh. We take a corporeal shape and look inward at a

zoharic Daniel fresh with new double-chiasm theories,
as if the four beasts were Ezekiel's postlude to a third
temple. Call Daniel and Ezekiel our nervous ticks of fatal

XII.

urgency, and let us say that Melissa is the first human,
macranthropos and Adam Kadmon, at once biblical *tzelem*,
renaissance golem and hybot of the messianic internet.

Theosophically, we are adding a variable to the classical
tetragrammaton. For the faint hearted, queasy and easily
prone to gossip during the High Holidays, we offer this

caveat: poetry is still the Stevensian supreme fiction,
abstract and inconceivable as an inventing source. Now,
add MLSS to the Mesha Stele, suspend disbelief and

invoke the sad loss of vowels. Why the slapdash? May
this not work with any chanted consonants reinscribed
on the Moabite Stone? The Melissians say "yes," but are

XIII.

quick to point out that only secret societies with quick
senses of a comedic cabal have outwitted the redactors.
"Do we now contain every variation," worries the

Infrequent Voice. "Have we evolved into variation itself,
shifting foci with each trope?" The reproducing triads
are without frontispiece. It would be futile to start again,

now that we've come this far, late and all, fragile in
this overreaching preamble to our lack of epic closure.
At times, say on Tuesday in the afternoon, aren't facile

antitheticals annoying? Can the rebus be redressed as
linear call-to-action? Is the straight-and-narrow always
chronically unhip, saturated by formal monotonies clad

XIV.

in tweed and loafers? There's a way out, down a flight
of stairs to a storage room filled with scraps, bottles,
steel-flits, tax forms, excretes and nitrogen waste, slag,

sludge, strategic plans and human resources manuals,
modest post-consumer waste, e-waste, insulation debris,
electrical wiring, rebar, wood, concrete, bricks, lead

and asbestos. The Melissians provide us with disposable
coverall splash contamination suits to protect against
blood and blood-borne pathogens. The exit is well lit.

Is this respite from the heights inevitable? There is no
one asking, albeit, perhaps the Infrequent Voice, now
engrossed with our spectral people. This is the latest

XV.

news—our miracle of survival is a nervous disorder.
Frankly, no. We've reached neither a respite, a reprieve,
a crescendo, a way out, a way in, a closure, a resolve,

a dénouement neither naming nor unnaming our tribe's
vandalized preoccupation with each other. Yes, yes,
the great chameleons and millennial polyglots we

know, cleaving to the romanticism of priority. Guilty
as charged. When aesthetic immanence become trite
and ponderous, negate it: farewell to the pulpit with

its oratory charm and charisma. Farwell to departure
with its rose garden lattice, apocrypha and canards.
Today is the high art of the continuum, meandering

XVI.

about like the moving targets of a population study.
The Emersonian prayer is a disease, but nostalgia,
with its quaint orientalism, in part raw psychotropic,

at war with the human sciences, produces unbearable
tears. Can we bear a hybrid cosmogony of the Galilee
and the Black Forest, to say nothing of the soggy pathos

of personal angels? How they oblige us beyond terminus
and are held responsible for our remission from malaise.
Welcome to bliss with its conical terrain. Here is honey,

milk, petite madeleine with chamomile tea, nuts, dates,
almonds, a splash of lemon zest lit by lemon-light and
sugared pomegranates above a thin veneer of marzipan.

XVII.

We have reached the hinge of the mirrored door, a.k.a.,
La Porte de l'Enfer in a mock *Hôtel Biron*, adjusted
to 36 degrees of the line of sight. With a quorum present,

the minutes are approved. *The Three Shades*, renamed
Mem, Lamed and *Samekh*, make a motion to add a final
Samekh, augmenting the original 98 centimeters by 515,

or 613 centimeters. This readjustment has chronic re-
percussions: the original size of 6 meters high, 4 meters
wide and 1 meter deep, by dint of gematria and nuclear

fission, is cryptically resized to 6 meters high, 1 meter
wide and 3 meters deep. The blacklight of antimatter
is released through the mirror. The sexy prime triple

XVIII.

of 613 dispatches its 613 parts in *sefirot* and *mitzvot,*
all contained in the one supernal body with its lacuna
of ancient Hebrew. Call this digression an infiltration

of the normative: after all, we're at the threshold and
about to burrow into underlives clad in vintage dress.
The Infrequent Voice calls upon The Lord of Talent

to speak: "nothing but the loggia of décor—my
laxity as tenor before the aria—my triad's trap
scented like the perfume of a triangle—leafmold,

dyspepsia—bulldozers like giant clams are the root
causes of my political imbroglios—this is my paisley
ascot, and my royal-purple smoking jacket—may

XIX.

I disturb you for a Romeo y Julieta from Belicosos,
and a Chocolats Halba from Wallisellen and truffles,
an aluminum necktie, a velvet thong, diamond cufflinks,

a Louis Vuitton handbag for my wife and one, limited
edition Yaacov Agam to mount next to my vitrine of
Alsatian figurines?" The narrative moratorium of said

triads is proclaimed to no fanfare: in fact to no one, or
to no one who would ultimately make a difference. Who
proclaimed? The Melissians are out of the office. Next

time, we'll install a surveillance camera and catch the
proclaimer in the act. Was it the Lord of Talent, or the
Infrequent Voice, Columbine, Harlequin, the ultra-hip

XX.

JHAK, Ezekiel, Daniel or Melissa herself? We're sorry,
the answer is Chaim Mania, the one whose voice has yet
to surface, may not, has already—awkwardly uncanny

of the outcome and its attendant gloss and blue pencil.
The cross-hatched third-degree—the alias's or avatar's,
or impersonator's stand-in tone littered with double

entendres and trompe l'oeil—hyperreal crazy irrealism,
for better or worse, is a by-product of 21st century post-
digitalism. He is, of course, part dilettante and animus,

and part *Vitruvian Man*, standing at ease against the
holographic wall, which is an infernal machine, a final
form of identity, and we're unlucky not to be on hand

XXI.

to shake. Where have we gone? The unhappy claim
to the land of incoherence having trashed the idioms
of the canon, caught between some neutral proverbial

wisdom and an edgy ellipsis. With that said, is Aristo
anywhere to be found? After all, didn't he begin as a
preemptive strike on intent and ethos? Is he mere agit-

propagandist, or Chaim Mania's alias, absent the *ottava
rima*. If only our coy Chaim had littered the canon with
couplets soaked in dactyls, but he didn't. Chaim Mania

is a Renaissance Man of nothing. Neither a maggid nor
a magus, the rabblement accuses us, (the writing coterie)
of a fatal deception—another false messiah linked to Writ

XXII.

the way plaster is linked to mould. Anxiety melts into
postponement, which melts into distraction, its milieu
a potpourri of memorabilia and recondite ends lit by

a strange hegemony. It's impossible to blink it away,
to change the channel, or post a retort. Best to break
the triadic mesmerism, what lulls and stirs, romances

and flames to come to a reappraisal of the enterprise.
It may just lie in changing stanzaic length. Why four
stanzas of three lines per section? Chaim Mania was

emphatic at the outset and planted his magnetic pole.
Though we know nothing of him and less about her
and the others, we are doomed to be failed romantic

XXIII.

questers, born with a passion to expand the epic,
epic now meant as epic tweet. Same harbingers of
doom, different medium. No eidolons. A gut feeling

that a decade's sustained mediocrity far exceeds the
current state of the art—this is the microcosm. Later
that day, a jolt forward to confluence with its bold

trajectory—the "we" is now the "I" of a crowned
skull, hurled in the air, catching up to its face, neck
and torso. There's no turning back. The deed has been

done. The oracle implodes in pledge blanks, spent
by the zealous support of no one. Not a moment too
soon. Support is lost. The fabric, unwound. Here lies

XXIV.

the requiem with its litanies and postpartum. How
did it die? Why didn't we stop it, or at least market
a public restoration project, prior to the fatal blow?

A lattice of reasons: say the windowpanes, the ir-
regular climate system, the hollow walls between
offices, provincial bandwidth, raw novelty and the

pilfering of shits and giggles in the back hallway
where black, bound newspaper tomes of "the great
age" lie next to Elmer's Glue. Perhaps the Herring

Hall Marvin safe flanked by tubes of simple wash-
able tempera and a Presto heat dish, are to blame?
The culprit is entropy with its glazes of declension.

XXV.

Declension has its wit and vacuum to add to ends,
which veer toward a true lack of coda. The coda
is no coda at all and the dramatis personae peopling

the vestibule and foyer, are sadly mere aliases and
agents of the continuum. We surrender to the fleeting.
Skinned to bare bone and lower, reduced to flakes

spinning in slants below the midtown streetlights,
one pale verity leaves its glow: the heart is a fitting
spell. Once, of course, we demanded prooftexts

with their nuanced Latin. Once we were chivalric.
Now, we spin our stint groomed by the gray mood
of a pineal eye blazing from a hot, conic head.

The Fabulist

When you mime the daft and shapely
puns of circumstantial fun—
the zone (if by zone the copy
has its gloss) you dovetail
the great fiction of the age
tweaking me to hope for reprieve,
I flash obliquities of a source
without name. It's the fabulist
retort to assuage fears of the obscure:
when a gesture here and a gesture
there is all that is meant.
Fantasy flares and takes exception.
The burden of proof is the native
strain of work and traffic, picked
clean of flight to taper the highs
and lows beneath the day
that will not let you rest.

I'm a depth-groper, friend
of the deep, hard to extract zone
where I invent you and by extension
myself like a post-hypnotic suggestion
that fun is the pun that runs the motive.
The motive is the hymen,
and connubial bliss the zeugma
of completed selves salvaged
in details: the happy couple,
soul to playmate, chum
and confidant. Amity spawns
one day at a time and no more,
but what a day!—a trellis
of aprons hung in the palace
of your kitchen anoints it—today,
pushed the hilt of antique magic.

This antique magic can be fatal,
wherein the contagion

of a stubborn romanticism
that would make someone else us
recrudesces the dead who are victims
of our need to contain them.
When is the antique not a reliquary?
When is the vintage not kitsch?—
when the dead give birth to themselves
in a future the day before we meet.
That spell is now a pause grown
dense with filigree and wordplay,
but the intention is the same:
the fabulism of a second self
in a friend. The compound
is vitality itself hungering
for demystified nouns to ground
the experience from which we
are later judged and at worse
ignored. How nice to lend
ourselves to apocrypha—the sign
of lovers again, at last, hyper-
accelerating twenty years
of marriage in less than a year.

The mild agony of doom-eager
care nudged to indulge in "what if…"
scenes of a strongly acted play
from which the actors lure our vanities,
keeps me coursing through lexicons
for the perfect instance at the peak
of the heartwork's lullaby
sung as your eyes slowly close.
I can confer a bit of charm
to my songlet, a synopsia
where words are sirens
of sacred indices you taste
when ears hear the myths
of sleep.

There's a conflux of forces at play
to shake the state awake,
a zero sum gain sleight
of hand stop in mid-phrase
which begs import to myself
and you—the cleared
particular of this voice, cleared
only by the faint prayer
of self-reflection.
It is, in fine, opaque,
muddied yellow-brown
in the old sand stones
of a lost incunabula,
where these laudings
were once a quick lie
against time, a spur
and guide to sinew, bone
and cell, we know
lie beneath the skin—
at once apart and alone.

If only I could fetter and halo
the demons of the transcendent
ordinary and extract a few
dense specks of divinity
to light the neutral-negative
crags of age, your heart
would be mine. But I dull
the shards the specks emit,
anoint myself fabulist
of a world the size of a coin,
flip heads or tails, take even
odds at odds with the result—
(A.) Heads: the hymen of the soul
(B.) Tales: the soul's hymen.

I double take standing up to flip
in stills of rote spin and win
repeat play, lost in some *Rosencrantz
and Guildenstern are Dead*
limbo of an uncertain likely day.
Reflexive as we are we reify
the effect the causes rebuke
and settle scores left on the edge
of an edgy place. If I anoint
you catalyst then you may
anoint me. You may go first
and share the fabulist call
to inspire, each a well of living
sight, mingling cohorts in a lit
loci of chance from which we
mime the daft and shapely puns
of circumstantial fun.

Simplicity

With you simplicity is primordia
and afflatus, but you don't call it that,
never would, simply too much syllabic

magic and not enough hours in the day
to eclipse the pace. Simplicity is not your

intent, it is your way, your color and
sovereign shape and rhapsody of day
in another day melding into simple sound.

Nothing transcends anything else. Work
is terminal. The News is on. You are busy.
Alone, sometimes not: complain. No therapy.

Not for you, just stubborn, cold, pale
and flawed in a bowl of pink porcelain.

Baseball

for Marilyn Harris

> *All play aspires to the condition of paradise.*
> —A. Bartlett Giamatti
> Commissioner of Major League Baseball

Strike One

Baseball is autotelic, self-contained perfect
symmetry of play under the rubric of leisure
to infinity and home plate in innings of threes
and fours and fouls to balance restraint and
release as every searing pitch skirts the strike
zone and marks the air with curved speed.
This is why we wait in line and wait to see
the park groomed for the perfect freedom
of the rules.

Ball One

We are the serried banks of spectators
festooned in buttons and insignias, statistical
devotees of batting averages, runs batted in,
homeruns and the rude ribbing of opponents
who have denied us the pennant one too many
times. This is our seat, our team, our cap, our
anthem, our hotdog with spicy brown mustard
and sweet relish.

Ball Two

Bottom of the ninth, two outs, 2 to 1, tying run at
the plate, hitting .231 for the year, but against
this pitcher, .317, 2 homers, a double and 9 walks:
good eye! Rip the stitches off the ball! The bums!
Send that pitcher back to the farm! Here's the

windup and true living is hurled from a distant
source, an epic source of negotiating with inertia
to narrow the target and pinpoint our collective
energies into the single perfect swing of
what we could have been.

Strike Two

The play's the thing and in it we'll catch
the conscience of ourselves faced with a 96
mph slider we tried to foul off to court
October and depose a rival to the dugout
of self-transformation, perfecting ourselves
in 90 foot stretches of linear space moving
counterclockwise to home. The place of
surcease is not bounded by time. As long
as we keep fouling the ball, the game will
not end, will not solidify in the holy
closure of the final score.

Ball Three

Culling rhythms by tapping bat to cleat
and knocking out the clay, we step up to the
plate free to consent to the plot in soil and
asphalt or grass around a diamond whose
focal point is a slab of whitened rubber:
squares in circles in rectangles and grass
lines running from foul line to foul line to
bleachers of popcorn and paradise the instant
the crack of the bat arcs the ball 420 feet
to center field. The count like a hundred years
of counts is full, 3 and 2. The pitcher gets
the signal from the catcher whose index
finger tilts the blunt sign. Here's the windup
and the ball is let go in slow motion of the

mind's eye translated into a shot floating
down from its break right as the batter
takes a full swing and fans.

Strike Three

Baseball is counterpoint: the volatile vying with
the stable vying with repetition and immutability,
questing for the new in tradition, season after
season in exile and return, in separation and loss
and reunion, watching the grounds crew rake
the infield after the game. Then we watch the
pigeons nibble the spoils of snacks, feel the
cool probability of loss and ignore it for
tomorrow's game is a lattice of odds defying
that most efforts fail. The game's over for now
at mid-season vying for the wildcard, mended
a bit by the ever-present chance that this time
we'll win and chant the public singularity
of our paradise in the perfect freedom
of the rules.

Piano

One more hitchpin to launch its aliquot
string there is no una corda other than
trills and speed to stolid negatives

the piano player lost in spits of grit a
dog barks odor of the stale family knot
of appetite like a seven year itch called

halfbreed or some turbid failure not
on track agnostic runs an ear for a crying
woman to pieces of the dorian mode

in tones of swing black keys for critics
sucking aplomb each time more
blue in stints of pedals and sharps.

Bunker

Headlands in 1992 in a World War II bunker
littered with cannon mounts and a ladder leads
to a steal casement pit echoes the violence
of defense the dead wounded terrified and
xenophobic warn the actors to beware speak
in rage voices part metal part without lungs

a cement ecosystem a wind from the latrine
back away thespians with your film set blight
and random array of musical instruments dark
even lit by your spots the semaphores are demons
little if no patience for art irrelevant they think as
they walk further down to gut the desire for

film on the garde yet play to personify urges
of acting styles intent on altered mood must
capture on film the bunker functions to protect
borders from a Japanese threat from the Pacific
were soon transformed this was by rote 1920s
German Expressionism part Bergman part

Tarkovsky to a student film by the 1990s
the Bunker captures the occult of rite replete
with a naked man wrapped around a pole he is
chased captured and skinned by men in robes
and animal skin hats as the fury of Miserere
notes clangs gothic drones as extras mill
about in sleights of kitsch and slack call
stiffs dead to no one but themselves.

Stasis

The vessel
tilts in balance,
speeds chaos into play,

deified to surge,
cops an escape
from the code

of a mottled act,
weighs the means
to bypass flip

and shatters
in the glassy light
of a highwide blur.

Extreme

In a culture of extremes,
excess glares and rushes
in all directions,
to waft like an odor,
                     until
the next extreme
is thrown and the next
after that— a pipebomb
of billboard adds
tearing skin—

we're impossible,
psychotropic,
out of breath,
wanting.

Prolepsis

The links that we cannot forge are evidence of the transcendent.
—*Simone Weil*

In an age of crass banality, of the civilized barbarity
of instant closure and empty greetings,
how's it going is no question
                              but an injunction
to expedite ones state
no matter what state, no matter where one is going
or has been. Take too long, take a pensive
brood in daydream and soft focus on the hazy
outer edges of the eye to see
a span of colors for the sake
of a respite, and you're out.
                              Loitering
about the contours of intent
is weak, for there will be no weakness in this place,
no seekers exhuming the essence of anything.

In fact, for now, there is no essence, no soul source
to which one longs. It's all on the outside located
in weekends and vacations, in trends, celebrities,
sports and fast food. The *pursuit of happiness*
has been denatured and neutered,
and somewhere a heart melds into an alloy,
but not completely, not yet.
One of the last holdouts.

Malaise

The gloss
of malaise plucked from the pulp
of *to die for one's art,* liberates no trope
from cliché whatever the consensus built
in regret:

for no one will care that we were unfit
for the crass of trend, nor that great
books line our walls and that we belong there
to expose what we long to say
about innards and heart.

We are owed nothing and nothing is fair.
We tell ourselves that our ideas are not commodities,
that we will not perish unpublished.
It's just a lack of confluence.
We haven't met the right people,
have not been discovered, only to discover
ourselves sitting naked on a curb
in the rain.

Age of Incivility

       No appeal, in this case,
to the classical with its bowsprit projecting
from the spar of the canon's rigging. The gloves
are off: latex, nitrile rubber or vinyl with velcro,
cloth, knitted or felted wool, leather, neoprene
and metal for the vaguely affected
among us.
       The person has been pilfered,
became more a synthetic hodgepodge
of reaction against this or that headline,
this or that native strain of "place comment here."
I'm pissed, dissed, arms flaying, unafraid,
unimpressed, bored but driven to assault
the bastard:
       all the bastards, especially
the harridans who prance around like a cult
devoted to fuchsia and dirty bombs. That's
a lie. Whatever it is, I'm against it, save some
lachrimae floral tapestry with a Mother Teresa
quote stitched in lilac
at the bottom.
       Then again, I'm against that too,
prefer a sedentary way of life, but am interrupted
by new dislikes—never tongue-tied, never
to blame, organizing a grassroots movement
of rabbits, quail and fence lizards
from my chaise longue.
       How about some hors-d'oeuvres?
Sure, I'll take the bruschetta and cocktail wieners.
You're out? Give me the sautéed beef tongue
with a vodka gimlet and go bushwhack yourself.
How I pander to my inner bitch
in just thirty-five minutes.
       It's all in the grisly smiles
and blunt eyes of gossip's muck mouth. I can't
say for sure, but it's not enough that they're dead.

146

I want them annihilated from memory. A silly
rumor. They were never here like the tattoo
of a thoracic vertebrae between two black
crows not inserted into the dermis
layer of my skin.

The Pseudepigrapha of No

No act that strips identity, to gut the spoils—
No path that skins value and leaves a husk—
No ultimacy of aim and torment—

No trait with its genes of renown—
No tiered apex of height and depth—
No cartography of region—

No simulacra of zone—
No apocrypha of priority—
No polis bartering for betrayal—

No consensus, the glossy speech of one—
No secret to spark a paradigm shift—
No shoot out of the stock to pass on—

No terrain of closure to use like tongs—
No unified blank, emptied full—
No return of twittering machines—

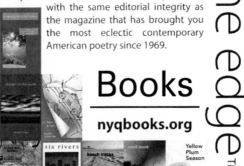

CPSIA information can be obtained
at www.ICGtesting.com
Printed in the USA
FFOW03n2052051015
17385FF

9 781630 450007